EMERGENT COMMONWEALTH

HUTCHINSON'S UNIVERSITY LIBRARY
POLITICS

EDITOR:
PROFESSOR G. D. H. COLE
Chichele Professor of Social and Political Theory in the University of Oxford

EMERGENT COMMONWEALTH
The British Colonies

by

W. E. SIMNETT
M.B.E.

FOUNDING EDITOR OF "THE CROWN COLONIST"
(NOW "NEW COMMONWEALTH")

HUTCHINSON'S UNIVERSITY LIBRARY
Hutchinson House, London, W.1.

Melbourne Sydney Auckland Bombay
Cape Town New York Toronto

First Published - 1954

325.342
S592e

Hist.
Feb. 23 1958.

Printed in Great Britain by
William Brendon & Son, Ltd.
The Mayflower Press (late of Plymouth)
at Bushey Mill Lane
Watford, Herts.

CONTENTS

	Preface	vii
Chapter I	Empire into Commonwealth	9
II	The Colonies Grow Up	16
III	The Caribbean and Atlantic	24
IV	The African Continent	44
V	The Mediterranean and Indian Oceans	79
VI	Malaya and The East	93
VII	The Pacific Islands	104
VIII	The Central Machinery	113
IX	Colonial Government and Service	126
X	Colonial Policy and Problems	139
XI	Future Trends	160
	Bibliography	169
	Postscript	181
	Index	183
	Selected List of Books Available in this series	187

PREFACE

WHEN invited to contribute this volume to the University Library, I looked again at the book on the British Colonial Empire which I was impelled to write after returning from a Government mission to the United States at the end of 1940. At that time no general introduction to the subject on those lines existed, and my experience both in America and earlier in conducting a Colonial journal here convinced me that something of the kind was urgently needed. The book was published in this country in 1942 and later separately in America, but although a new British edition extensively revised was issued in 1948, events in the Colonial field move so fast nowadays that it is already to some extent out of date. Even the title would today be regarded as obsolete or obsolescent.

The present work has accordingly been written afresh on a somewhat different plan, and although, even since the manuscript was completed, some changes have occurred which are indicated in the Postscript, it may be taken that both these and any later changes will be part of the steady advance of the main groups and countries towards self-government within the Commonwealth—hence the Emergent Commonwealth—and in broad outline and essential fact this volume should remain accurate for many years to come. As and when new editions are required, details can readily be brought up to date. Within the scope of this series, only an introduction can be attempted to a very great subject which deserves and will repay further study, and this the Bibliography is designed to assist.

I would like to express my thanks to Sir Alan Pim, to Professor G. D. H. Cole, and as always to my wife for her constant help, criticism and encouragement.

W.E.S.

CHAPTER I

EMPIRE INTO COMMONWEALTH

IT is desirable at the outset to clarify certain terms which appear to be variously understood. In some quarters it is still customary to speak of the British Empire when what is meant is the British Commonwealth of nations, or briefly the Commonwealth. A variant which is often heard is the Commonwealth and Empire, the double term being apparently thought necessary in order to include specifically those territories which are not yet self-governing and equal partners in the Commonwealth. These territories, the colonies or dependencies of the United Kingdom, are sometimes collectively referred to as the British Colonial Empire, a phrase which is obsolescent if not already obsolete. "Commonwealth and Empire" is not strictly necessary, since the dependencies of member nations are included with them in the Commonwealth. "Dominion" is another term which is passing into disuetude, the various countries being referred to simply by name or as members of the Commonwealth. In any case Great Britain is equal with the others, being *primus inter pares* only in recognition of her special position as "founder" member. "Colony" and "dependency" are also terms, with the subordinate status thereby implied, which are destined to pass away in time.

The British Commonwealth of nations is the subject of an earlier volume in this series, but that work dealt only with what may be called the senior partners in the Commonwealth, namely, the United Kingdom, Canada, Australia, New Zealand, South Africa, India, Pakistan, and Ceylon. Southern Rhodesia and Eire were also referred to, but the former, although a self-governing colony, did not hold full "dominion" status; it now forms part of the Central African Federation. Eire is not a member of the Commonwealth, although its republican form of government does not exclude it, since two great republics are full members of the Commonwealth, and Ireland as a whole is certainly a "mother country" in the same sense as Great Britain. But until Irishmen of the North and South come to some mutual understanding and agreement, and past history no longer divides a natural geographic entity, Eire will presumably remain in its present somewhat anomalous position, though there is nothing to prevent it seeking entry (or re-entry) into the Commonwealth at any future time.

The Commonwealth today, however, may be regarded as including not only the senior partners, the fully independent and equal sovereign nations voluntarily associated together, but also the junior partners or colonies and other dependencies. It is the latter which form the subject of the present volume, and which we describe as the emergent Commonwealth.

These territories, some thirty-five in number, large and small, strung across the globe and covering an area of some 2,000,000 square miles with a population of about 75,000,000 people of all races, colours and creeds, have no formal relation with the Commonwealth as a whole, but only with Great Britain (except for those few which are dependencies of other Commonwealth countries). On her part Great Britain regards herself as trustee for the future of these peoples, and the long-declared objective of her colonial policy is to prepare them for eventual self-government within the Commonwealth. Trusteeship is indeed already verging into partnership, and no strict dividing line can now be drawn between senior and junior partners. It is but a short time since Ceylon was the premier Crown colony, but almost overnight and quite peaceably, it became a fully self-governing country and a senior partner in the Commonwealth. The smoothness and ease of its transition presented a striking contrast to the mutual troubles of its greater neighbours on the mainland, India and Pakistan, before they settled down to independent nationhood.

With the growth of political awareness and the rising ferment of nationalism among dependent peoples, colonial status, that is, the political subordination of one country or people to another, is fast becoming an anachronism, and whilst the political and economic advancement of the more primitive and backward peoples may yet take some time, it may be said that the phase of empire and of colonies which has subsisted in various forms throughout the long history of mankind, at last shows signs of coming to an end, and "colony" and "colonials" are terms destined to pass away with the eventual attainment of political independence by the present dependent peoples of the world.

In this transition from empire to commonwealth, from domination or tutelage to free association, Great Britain has led the way; and in order to understand the position of the present British colonies, it is desirable to sketch in briefly the historical background, more especially as the present oversea senior partners in the Commonwealth were originally colonies or dependencies of Great Britain.

It is sometimes said that Great Britain acquired her empire in a fit of absence of mind, though a far less charitable view has been taken of the process by various other nations. The building up of the empire was in fact so far from being the outcome of any consistent or deliberate policy that we lost the most potentially important part of our first empire, the thirteen American colonies, through the shortsightedness and ineptitude of our politicians at the end of the eighteenth century. America might otherwise have become the first and greatest British Dominion with incalculable effect on the subsequent history of the world, but Alexander Hamilton of Bermuda, who suggested this solution in precisely those terms, and who later signed the Declaration of Independence, was, alas, too far in advance of his time. Whether history will ever be reversed and America re-enter the Commonwealth as its leading member remains to be seen.

We have learned that dearly bought lesson thoroughly since (though many Americans have apparently not yet realized this), but in those days, it must be remembered, all colonizing nations regarded their colonies or "plantations" as *possessions* to be exploited primarily for the benefit of the metropolitan country responsible for their administration and defence, and without much regard for the wishes or interests of their inhabitants. Amongst those colonial powers, however, Great Britain, despite her early mistakes, has been on the whole the most liberal in her attitude and practice, and she gave outstanding evidence of this more liberal policy in her great humanitarian drive for the abolition of slavery throughout British territory.

The second British Empire grew up, mainly during the nineteenth century, in all manner of ways, by discovery, conquest, cession, treaty, requests for protection, settlement, or finally mandate. So little was it animated by the spirit of "grab" sometimes alleged against us by nations who displayed no undue hesitation in acquiring fresh territories, that there were many refusals or reluctant and tardy acceptance of responsibilities almost thrust upon us, and not a few retrocessions of territories gained in war, of which but one amongst many examples was the Netherlands Indies, ruled over for a brief period to their great advantage by Sir Stamford Raffles, the founder of Singapore and modern Malaya. The Congo was another country offered first to Britain and refused, and considering her prior opportunities for expansion in Africa had she been so inclined, instead of taking a foremost part in the subsequent "scramble", she may well be astonished at her own moderation, and that despite the extent of British territory in Africa today. Neither Raffles nor later would-be "Empire builders" got much countenance or encouragement from the home government of their day. Nevertheless, some not inconsiderable additions were due to individual or commercial enterprise, sometimes in the recognized form of chartered companies, whilst others resulted inevitably from our commanding sea power, and the necessity for coaling stations and guarding lines of communication across the world.

For the most part, the second empire was a fortuitous growth, naturally reflecting the predominant position of Britain in the nineteenth century and the wide-ranging enterprise of her inhabitants; but so far was it from a deliberate policy of expansion that in the sixties and seventies there was a movement at home to cut our oversea responsibilities and abandon what were then the colonies altogether. Fortunately, this did not succeed, but neither did the opposite movement for imperial federation under the leadership of Great Britain. Instead, the most striking political development of the latter part of that century was the steady growth towards full self-government of the white communities of Canada, Australia, and New Zealand and lastly of South Africa, until they finally reached Dominion or independent status after the First World War. This was a natural development, since these communities were akin to our own and had been bred in the same tradition; it had happened earlier in the American colonies, but now we had learned wisdom, and beginning with the Durham Report in Canada, instead of repressing, we encouraged the growth and thus took the first steps on the road which has led to the Commonwealth of today. The unification of South Africa and the reconciliation of Dutch and British was a wise act of enlightened statesmanship after the tragedy of the Boer war, whatever we may think of the present position in the subcontinent.

The evolution of the British Empire has therefore been centrifugal instead of centripetal, away from rather than towards any centralized political system, thus differing from empires in the past, and this process culminated in the Statute of Westminster of 1931, which gave formal recognition to what had been already achieved, and may be said to have brought to an end the second empire, and to have inaugurated the third era, in which the Empire has been and is being transformed into the Commonwealth.

The British Commonwealth set up under that statute was declared to consist of "autonomous communities within the British Empire in no way subordinate to one another in any aspect of their domestic or external affairs, though united by a common allegiance to the Crown and freely associated as members of the British Commonwealth of nations". In other words, each of these countries is a completely independent and sovereign state, bound to the others by no formal ties and associated together only by common sentiment or tradition. Great Britain is in this definition a Dominion like the rest, *primus inter pares* by historic precedence but having no formal power or influence over any other member of the Commonwealth, the Crown being the only common symbol and the monarch of Great Britain being equally but separately the constitutional head of the other member countries, being advised therein by Ministers and Governments responsible to independent Parliaments as at home.

It will be noticed that the Statute of 1931 spoke of "communities within the British Empire", thereby implying that the Commonwealth was not then coterminous or synonymous with the Empire, and indeed at that time the Indian and Colonial empires were beyond the formal scope of that statute, but India was already advancing on the road to self-government, and when, after the interruption of the Second World War, that was finally attained in 1945, although the sub-continent was divided into two independent countries, India and Pakistan, both states voluntarily took their place as senior partners or "autonomous communities" with the others in the Commonwealth. Indeed the resources of the Commonwealth proved flexible enough to produce a formula which satisfactorily associated the republican form of government with countries owing direct allegiance to the Crown, the monarch being formally recognized as Head of the Commonwealth. This left the way open for future accessions.

There then remained only the Colonial Empire, but the premier Crown colony, Ceylon, became a fully-fledged dominion and senior partner in the Commonwealth soon after the accession of India and Pakistan, and it was manifest that a status accorded to certain communities within a political system founded on the ideals and institutions of democracy could not logically be denied to others. Britain had indeed already tacitly recognized this by her policy of trusteeship for the colonies and her declared intention of preparing them for eventual self-government.

While some people still stubbornly speak of the Empire, or like Sir Winston Churchill, of Commonwealth and Empire, the latter form is at best residual, and like Balzac's *peau de chagrin* shrinks with every political advance in the colonies, but instead of vanishing, assumes a new and better form. Sir Winston might declare that he would not "preside over the liquidation of the Empire", but already that empire was in irrevocable process, if not of "liquidation", certainly of transformation. But the British Empire is not breaking up: it is growing up!

All earlier empires had followed the orthodox pattern and inevitably had suffered decline and fall; the British Empire was the first to grow and transform itself peaceably into something unique in history. The Commonwealth is therefore probably the most interesting and startling political experiment that has ever been made, an experiment moreover that is still in progress: indeed the stage which it has now reached is perhaps the most important for its future development. For that reason and because in the last analysis that future depends upon ourselves, we should all take the keenest interest in it; yet the truth is that neither among the British public nor the overseas peoples is there any full knowledge or understanding of its implications or great potentialities.

As a political system, it has no logical or formal structure, and indeed in many ways is a mass of contradictions and anomalies. Accordingly it is entirely incomprehensible to foreigners, and Americans find it a strange and difficult conception compared with the clear-cut precision of their own written federal constitution. But it is in its very lack of precision or even definition that is to be found its strength and adaptability. When a new situation has to be met, an empirical solution is usually found without too much regard as to whether it fits into any coherent or logical plan.

The British have never been logicians. They ask of any arrangement, however anachronistic, contradictory or nebulous, not whether it is reasonable, but does it or will it work? The Commonwealth is theoretically impossible; in practice it works surprisingly well. It has within it the seeds of organic growth and the possibility of expansion, and may yet prove the nucleus and pattern for a new world order based on free association and mutual co-operation.

CHAPTER II

THE COLONIES GROW UP

IT is against this background that we have now to consider the present British colonies or the emergent Commonwealth. They are all, except perhaps the most primitive and isolated communities, in process of transition, and since self-government is the goal for all, there can be no prolonged halting-place on the road and no strict dividing line between these colonies and the countries that have already attained adult nationhood within the Commonwealth. Even as we write, one after another is coming to political maturity and each will take its place with the other senior partners as "autonomous communities" until there are no longer senior and junior partners, but, however diverse their individual economies and circumstances, equal political members of a world-wide Commonwealth of nations.

Before that time, there will have to be serious consideration of the measure of responsibility of the more advanced members of the Commonwealth for the welfare of their less politically and economically advanced brethren. At present Britain is alone responsible for the British colonies, and politically that trust is inescapeable, but it would seem appropriate, especially as more countries graduate to full partnership, that they should take a more active interest in the welfare of the remaining "juniors". The Colombo Plan is a great step forward in this direction and its scope is by no means confined to backward countries of the Commonwealth, but "colonialism" everywhere, and its eventual abrogation, is indeed a collective responsibility of civilization and not of the present colonial powers alone.

The British Commonwealth as a whole covers some 13,000,000 square miles or nearly a quarter of the earth's surface, and its aggregate population is about 600,000,000, which is roughly a quarter of the world's inhabitants. It extends over the five continents and around the seven seas, and from

THE COLONIES GROW UP

the North to the South Pole, although the bulk of its peoples occupy tropical or sub-tropical latitudes. In numbers it is predominantly a coloured Commonwealth, a fact which all would do well to bear constantly in mind. Within its boundaries, it contains a large proportion of the raw materials and economic wealth of the world, and in many areas these natural resources are still undeveloped or only in the early stages of development. Potentially, and considered as a whole, it is probably the richest and most powerful community of nations in the world. Other volumes in this series have dealt with the principal members of this great community; we are concerned here, as already stated, with 2,000,000 out of the 13,000,000 square miles and with some 75,000,000 people, white, black, brown, and yellow, of whom only the small minority are Europeans.

These widely scattered territories were originally known as Crown colonies to distinguish them from the self-governing colonies which later became Dominions, but the term is now falling into disuetude. Moreover, many were not colonies but protectorates and mandated territories. The term also applied, as we shall see, to a particular form of government or administration, but that also has been and is being modified in many cases to approximate to varying measures of representative government. Indeed the term "dominion" itself has not escaped the spirit of change which affects the whole Commonwealth. Originally proposed by Canada as an alternative to kingdom or realm in deference to the supposed sensitivity of its southern neighbour, it is now thought in some quarters, quite unwarrantedly, to imply something less than the status of the United Kingdom. "Realm" was again favoured, though this could obviously not apply to the two great republics, but it is usual now to refer to the member countries by their names *sans phrase*, and even to drop the adjective British in speaking of the Commonwealth, except on formal or particular occasions as between certain individual members. Incidentally, the Australian federation is itself a commonwealth, but so, for that matter, is Massachusetts!

The oldest British colonies are those in the Caribbean or West Indies group, and it is surprising today that these were once considered as of greater importance than the thirteen young settlements on the American mainland. Sugar was then king. They comprise the island groups of Jamaica, Trinidad and Tobago, the Bahamas, Barbados, and the Leeward and Windward Islands, and on the mainland British Honduras in Central America, and British Guiana in South America. Bermuda, farther north, is not a part of the West Indian group. In the North Atlantic are St. Helena and Ascension, and in the South Atlantic the "loneliest island" of Tristan da Cunha, whilst near the toe of South America are the Falkland Islands with their dependencies stretching towards the South Pole.

In area, the British colonies in the great continent of Africa comprise over 80 per cent of the whole, and while extent of territory is by no means the sole measure of political and economic importance (else Great Britain itself would cut but a small figure in the world), the British African territories fill a very prominent place in the colonial scene, and provide most of the problems which concern us today.

On the West coast of Africa around the "bulge", are the four British territories of the Gambia, Sierra Leone, the Gold Coast, and Nigeria, separated from each other by intervening French territory, the last-named being a huge country four times the size of Great Britain and with a population of some 30,000,000. Joined administratively with the Gold Coast is that portion of the former German Togoland mandated to Great Britain, and with Nigeria is included a similar strip of the Cameroons, the larger portions of both territories being mandated to France.

The East African group comprises Kenya, Uganda and Tanganyika, and the sultanate of Zanzibar (with Pemba) off the mainland. Tanganyika, which is slightly larger than Nigeria, though much more thinly populated, forms the larger part of the former German East Africa. Stretching to the north of this group is the vast territory of the Sudan, nearly 1,000,000 square miles in extent. It was administered by Britain under a condominium with Egypt, and the small band of British officials who constituted the Sudan political service under the Foreign Office, transformed this huge country from the chaos and ruin in which it was left after the defeat of the Mahdi into a peaceful, prosperous and progressive community which they prepared for self-government, continuing their devoted service up to the end. The Sudan has many serious problems to face on entry into independence, but it owes a lasting debt to the foundations laid by its British administrators. It is a story of which Britain may justly be proud, but although brief reference is made to it later, the Sudan was never, of course, part of the colonial empire.

Below the East African group come the associated territories of Northern and Southern Rhodesia and Nyasaland, which now form the Central African Federation. South West Africa was mandated to South Africa and now forms an integral part of the Union. Adjoining or embedded in Union territory are the three British protectorates of Bechuanaland, Basutoland and Swaziland, which it was intended should eventually, subject to the consent of their inhabitants, be transferred to the Union. The last British territory in Africa is British Somaliland, isolated on the "horn" of Africa, bordering the Gulf of Aden.

The three British outposts in the Mediterranean are Gibraltar, Malta, and Cyprus, the first-named being a fortress and a municipality rather than a colony. Cyprus in the Eastern Mediterranean is close to Asia Minor, where formerly Britain had wide responsibilities. In the First World War, she had conquered Mesopotamia, most of Syria, and Palestine and Transjordan; at that time Egypt was a British protectorate, but became an independent kingdom in 1922. Mesopotamia remained for some years under British mandate, but was granted independence in 1931 and became the present Arab state of Iraq. Syria, after the British had cleared most of the country, was mandated to the French, but is now also independent. There remained the mandated territories of Palestine and Transjordan. The latter is now the independent state of Jordan. In Palestine, the Balfour Declaration had favoured the establishment of a national home for the Jews, but owing to the conflicts of Arabs and Jews, complicated by the Jewish problem in the Second World War, the British administration had a troubled and stormy history, terminated by the relinquishment of the mandate and the setting up of the present state of Israel. The only British territory now remaining in this region is the colony of Aden at the mouth of the Red Sea and its protectorate, including the Hadhramaut, stretching across the southern coast of Arabia.

In the Indian Ocean we have the island groups of Mauritius and the Seychelles, and rounding the Indian peninsula with Ceylon at its base, we come to the Federation of Malaya and the colony of Singapore. On the great island of Borneo are the three territories of British North Borneo, Brunei and Sarawak, and off the coast of China, the colony of Hong Kong. In this region, Australia is responsible for Papua and the territory of New Guinea, and New Zealand for Western Samoa. Throughout the Pacific, there are many scattered island groups, such as the Fiji group and the Western Pacific High Commission, comprising the British Solomons, the Gilbert and Ellice groups, the protected kingdom of Tonga, Nauru, the New Hebrides (an Anglo-French condominium), Pitcairn, Cocos-Keeling islands and others.

Thus we have made a circuit of the British colonies from the greatest to the smallest round the world. There is now no sharp distinction between fully or largely self-governing colonies and those that are at varying pace advancing towards that goal. Ultimate responsibility rests with the Colonial Office in London, of which the political head is the Secretary of State for the Colonies, who is a member of the Cabinet. In the last analysis therefore, the Parliament and electorate of this country are responsible for the colonial peoples. But the colonies are not governed from Whitehall. Each colony has its own government headed by the Governor, who represents the Crown and is nominated by the Secretary of State. Although he possesses reserved powers, these are seldom used in practice, and government is conducted through the executive and legislative councils, which vary in composition and mode of election or nomination in the different colonies. The actual administration is carried on by the Colonial Service, a unified body whose members in the higher ranks at least are liable to serve anywhere in the colonies (and from whom Colonial Governors are as a rule selected), but who act locally under the authority of the Governor in council.

Attached to the Colonial Office are various expert advisers, committees and other bodies to assist and advise the Secretary of State in his complex task. The Crown Agents, who are also under the authority of the Secretary of State, act for all Colonial Governments as purchasing agents in London and in various technical, commercial and financial capacities. Some Colonial governments maintain Commissioners and information offices in London. Trade Commissioners and commercial correspondents are also maintained by the Home Government in some of the colonies. Both the central and local machinery of government will be more fully described in a later chapter.

From the economic point of view, the British colonies considered as a whole are of great and growing importance. They already constitute one of the greatest oversea markets for British products, for the colonies are for the most part primary producers and have comparatively few industries of their own. In return for raw materials and foodstuffs, therefore, they are able to take an increasing range and volume of British manufactured goods. However, their total trade, considerable as it is today and rapidly as it has increased in the present century, is still capable of almost indefinite expansion, since the economic resources of many territories are as yet largely undeveloped, while the standard of living of the bulk of the inhabitants, at present very low, can be progressively raised as their productivity increases and demands for more than the primary necessities of life arise and can be satisfied. Already of course many communities are far ahead of others in this respect, but a comparatively slight increase in the standard of living of the more primitive communities would make a tremendous difference to the total volume of trade.

If a motto were sought for the colonial family, it might well be "Unity in diversity". Individually these territories are diverse in situation, size, population, government, race, and social and economic development. They are in a constant state of evolution and experiment, and of political and social development, but despite all differences, they exhibit an underlying and essential unity.

They share many conditions and problems, both physical and economic, in common, and although individual forms of government vary, certain broad principles are applicable to all. A body of expert knowledge and advice is being steadily built up at headquarters and made available to all; they are administered by a Service uniform in training and tradition and partly interchangeable in personnel. Finally, they are ultimately controlled and guided through the Colonial Office on the lines of a declared common policy, subject to supervision and criticism by the British Parliament. The central feature of that policy is the principle of trusteeship, which regards the interests of the colonial peoples as paramount and the objective as the eventual evolution of the best form of self-government of which the various peoples may prove capable.

This is a critical and transitional phase in the life-history of the colonial system generally. Politically, economically and socially, it is in a state of flux. What are termed the backward peoples and the countries under-developed by Western standards are in ferment and no community can remain isolated from the prevalent influences of change. So far as the British colonies are concerned, they were already on the move, though necessarily at varying pace according to their stage of development. In constitutional and social change, *festina lente* is an admirable maxim, but in the world as it is today, it cannot always be observed in practice.

We in this country have had the benefit of centuries of experience, but some colonial peoples may have to abridge those centuries to decades or less. This may have dangerous results, but the risk must be taken, for in the last analysis self-government is better than good government, if we cannot have both, and peoples must within reason be allowed to make their own mistakes. Our trust is for the permanent interests of the colonial peoples themselves, and our great endeavour must be, despite clamour in some quarters and amongst the more vocal but not necessarily typical elements in certain colonies, not to force the pace beyond that which in their true interests will enable them to evolve their own political pattern and to stand securely on their own feet in the conditions of the modern world. Already we have made some bold and daring experiments, and so far we have been justified in the event, but we cannot escape our responsibilities for these peoples whom we hope eventually to welcome as full partners in the Commonwealth.

THE COLONIES GROW UP

We have now to pass in review the individual colonies in their various geographical groups, to examine the machinery of central and local government, to consider some of their problems and their relations with other countries, and finally to indicate some possible trends of future development. Since this modest volume cannot hope to provide more than an introduction to the colonial world, a select bibliography is appended for the assistance of those who may wish to carry their studies further.

CHAPTER III

CARIBBEAN AND ATLANTIC COLONIES

In surveying the British colonies, it will be convenient to proceed from the Western hemisphere to the Far East and Pacific, and this is appropriate since the Caribbean group are amongst the oldest British "possessions" and were at one time regarded as the most important of all our dependencies. They have had a long and troublous history dating back to the seventeenth century and if in the future they are to take their rightful place in the Commonwealth, they must do so on some federal basis as a West Indian dominion, since individually or in separate groups, they would be too small economically or politically to subsist as independent units in the conditions of the modern world. Federation is what Britain desires for the West Indies, and the movement has already made great progress and gained a large measure of local support, though some difficulties and suspicions still remain to be overcome.

It has sometimes been suggested, though not in any responsible quarter, that the West Indies might prefer to be attached politically, since they are so near geographically, to the United States, but such suggestions could only have originated in complete ignorance of West Indian mentality and feeling. West Indians are proud of their British citizenship and membership of the Commonwealth and their just desire is to attain complete self-government within that ambit. Indeed it had to be made clear at the date of granting war-time bases to the United States forces, which was done in conjunction with the West Indian governments, that these were only leased, and that sovereignty was in no way affected. It would perhaps be more appropriate if a future West Indian Federation were to establish some special link with Canada, in view of the close trading interests between them.

The British West Indies form part of an archipelago which sweeps in a great semi-circular curve from Florida to the coast of South America, enclosing the Caribbean Sea. The British islands comprise Jamaica, Trinidad and Tobago, Barbados, the Leeward and Windward groups, and the Bahamas, which with Bermuda, over 500 miles north, though not formally part, may be included for convenience. With the islands are grouped the mainland colonies of British Honduras in Central America, and British Guiana in South America. Other Caribbean countries intermingled with the British group are Cuba (the largest), the island containing Haiti and San Domingo, Puerto Rico, a territory of the United States, and one or two small French and Dutch islands.

The West Indies appear in history from the discovery of individual islands by Columbus and other early navigators and their subsequent settlement or annexation by various European nations. Columbus landed on San Salvador in the Bahamas in 1492 and the Indies owed their name to his belief that he had reached India by a western route. English settlement began in St. Kitts in 1623. Many of the islands changed hands several times in the struggle for power along what was once the Spanish Main, and they are associated with many battles and naval engagements, and latterly with the name of Nelson and other commanders. The full story must be sought in histories of the period, or in the earlier volume in this series on the British West Indies.

The original inhabitants were a primitive race known as the Caribs, but these have virtually disappeared, and were succeeded by the African slaves poured in by European proprietors to cultivate the sugar plantations which were then the principal source of wealth. It is their freed descendants, with many admixtures from other races, who constitute today the bulk of the West Indian population, together with the local-born European families known as "Creoles". There is no colour bar in the West Indies.

The total population of the group including the mainland colonies exceeds 3,000,000, and in some of the islands, notably Barbados, it is growing fast, while the mainland colonies need many more inhabitants for adequate development. Most of the islands are notable for their scenic beauty, and nearly all are fortunate in possessing fertile soils capable of growing a wide range of the "kindly fruits of the earth". Much of this region, however, is subject to occasional hurricanes and earthquakes, though the southern-most islands escape the hurricane zone.

JAMAICA

This is the largest island of the British group, being some 145 miles in length and 50 miles in extreme breadth. The Cayman islands and Turks and Caicos islands to the south are dependencies of Jamaica. The population of the whole is nearly 1,500,000. The name derives from the native Xaymaca, well watered, which aptly describes this land of rushing streams, verdant scenery, and thick forests clothing the central range of the famous Blue Mountains.

The island remained in Spanish possession until it capitulated to a naval and military force sent by Cromwell in 1655. The old capital of Spanish Town and for many years Port Royal were the headquarters of the buccaneers who contributed greatly to the wealth of the colony, which later was further augmented by the slave trade. After an earthquake had overwhelmed Port Royal in 1692, Kingston, the present capital, took its place, and although that has also since suffered from earthquakes, it is now a populous city with fine public buildings. Other towns are Spanish Town, Port Antonia, Montego Bay, Falworthy, Port Maria, and Savanna la Mar.

Jamaica enjoys wide climatic variety and its products are equally varied, the chief being fruit, especially bananas and citrus, but the former has had to contend with a local disease which has now been eradicated. Other important exports are sugar, rum, coffee, cocoa, coconuts, pimento, ginger, and cinchona. Blue Mountain coffee is famous. There is a Government railway, an extensive system of roads, and air and steamship communication with Canada, the United States and Europe.

Jamaica's constitution was originally granted by Charles II in 1660 and lasted for over 200 years, but after an insurrection violently suppressed by Governor Eyre in 1865, which was the subject of much controversy, this was surrendered and Crown colony government was established. Since then, however, further progress has been made, and today Jamaica is virtually self-governing, having a legislature with a Speaker and its own responsible Ministers led by a Chief or Prime Minister, election being based on adult suffrage. The Governor still maintains the old Spanish title of Captain-General.

Trinidad and Tobago

together constitute one colony, Tobago (which is reputed to be "Robinson Crusoe's isle") having been united with Trinidad by Order in Council in 1888. Owing to its varied resources and industries, the colony is in many respects the most progessive, prosperous and cosmopolitan in the West Indies. It lies close to the mainland of South America, being about 16 miles east of Venezuela, and it is about 50 miles long by about 40 miles in average breadth. Tobago, 21 miles north-east of Trinidad, is 26 miles long by $7\frac{1}{2}$ miles at its greatest breadth. The joint population is about 700,000.

Discovered by Columbus in 1498, it has retained its original Spanish name and the capital is Port of Spain. Both islands have a chequered history. Each was settled in turn by Spanish, English, Dutch, and French, and all the colonists had to contend with the fierce Carib inhabitants. Both islands changed hands several times, but were ceded to the British Crown in 1802 and 1814 respectively. The climate of Trinidad is tropical, divided into a dry and wet season, and that of Tobago is very healthy: it has been called the Negro's paradise. In addition to Port of Spain, the principal towns are San Fernando, Mueurapo, Tunapuna, Princes Town, and Arima; and in Tobago, Scarborough.

As an economic unit, Trinidad is more stable than other islands because of its varied range of products, agricultural, mineral and industrial, and possibly also owing to its proximity to the mainland. It has also a greater racial admixture than the other islands, there being a larger proportion of persons of European, South American and East Indian birth or extraction. The island's most valuable single asset is the famous natural pitch lake, and it is also the largest producer of mineral oil in the colonies. The main exports are sugar, cocoa, coconuts, petroleum, asphalt, limejuice, and grapefruit. The Usine St. Madeleine is one of the largest sugar factories in existence, and many secondary industries are being developed.

An important institution located in Trinidad is the Imperial College of Tropical Agriculture, but this serves not only the West Indies generally but the colonies as a whole, training specialists and carrying out research work of great value throughout tropical countries.

Constitutionally Trinidad follows the pattern of Jamaica, but while the objective of the franchise was equally universal adult suffrage, the extremely mixed character of the population made it necessary to proceed by stages. Ministers are responsible for public business in a legislature consisting mainly of elected members. When federation is eventually set up, there will probably have to be a sharing of federal headquarters and functions between Jamaica and Trinidad.

BARBADOS

This small island, somewhat larger than the Isle of Wight, has been called the garden of the West Indies, and is proudly known by Barbadians as "Little England", because of its intensely English appearance and tradition. The landscape, with its small fields and trim cultivation, has all the appearance of the English countryside. It is however the most densely populated of the West Indian group, and as the population, at present approaching 250,000, is constantly increasing, this raises a problem of emigration. Many Barbadians emigrate to other islands and to the United States, but on the other hand the mainland colonies are in great need of more people for development; their highland areas are also suitable for white settlement.

Barbados has always been an English possession since the date of the first settlement in 1627, although its ownership was disputed between early groups of proprietors until it was formerly annexed to the Crown in 1662. Bridgetown, the present capital, was founded in 1628 and during the civil war in England a number of royalists settled in the island. The negroes, who constitute the great bulk of the population, are intelligent and industrious, but for the most part are desperately poor, although economic conditions are now steadily improving. The climate is bracing and the island is much visited as a health resort.

Barbados was once the premier colony of the Windward group, but in 1885 it was separated from the others and made a distinct government. Next to Bermuda, its legislature claims to be one of the oldest in the Commonwealth, but since the old planter families long retained effective control, the franchise was, until recent years, extremely restricted, excluding the bulk of the population. It has however, now been greatly extended and the legislature has become more representative of the community as a whole.

Sugar is still the staple product of the island, Barbados sugar like Demerara from British Guiana being of distinctive quality. The island is the home of Codrington College, founded by the old West Indian family of that name, which has a high reputation as an educational institution throughout the West Indies. It gives an education of university standard to all irrespective of colour and is affiliated to Durham University at home.

The Leeward Islands

The Leeward group consists of four presidencies, namely, Antigua with Barbuda, St. Kitts-Nevis with Anguilla, Montserrat, and the British Virgin islands. Dominica, which was formerly in the group, was transferred to the Windwards in 1939. The islands belong to the chain known as the Lesser Antilles, except the Virgin group which forms the eastern extremity of the Great Antilles. They were discovered by Columbus on his second voyage in 1493 and became British in the seventeenth century.

The islands were originally colonized from St. Kitts (St. Christopher) as centre, and they have always since been associated politically. They are under one Governor and since 1871 there has been one Executive and one Legislative Council for the four presidencies elected on the basis of adult suffrage, although each, except the Virgin islands, maintains a legislative council for local purposes. The general legislature comprises both official and elected members the latter being chosen by the elected members of the local councils: the Virgin islands member is appointed by the Governor.

The principal towns are St. John in Antigua, and Basseterre in St. Kitts. Antigua is the main island in the group, but St. Kitts has the distinction of being the oldest of the British Caribbean possessions, having been colonized by Sir Thomas Warner in 1623. Barbuda was long owned by the West Indian family of the Codringtons, who as previously mentioned founded the college in Barbados. Nevis, separated from St. Kitts only by a narrow sea passage, was united with it in 1882. It is known as Nelson's island, for here the great seaman was married, although it was at Antigua, in English Harbour, that he refitted his ships prior to the Battle of Trafalgar. Nevis was also the birthplace of Alexander Hamilton, author of *The Federalist* and one of the framers of the American Constitution, who had previously proposed that the American colonies should form an oversea British Dominion. From later residence, he is also claimed by Bermuda.

Montserrat, which more than once changed hands between British and French, was originally colonized by Irish settlers, and some of the negroes were long said to possess a noticeable Irish brogue! The Virgin islands were originally divided between Britain and Denmark, but the Danish islands, their only possession in the West Indies, were purchased by the United States in 1916. The British group number about thirty small islands, the chief being Tortola (containing the principal centre, Roadtown), Virgin Gorda and Anegada. They are probably the least known of all the British West Indies.

The population of the Leeward group is round about 150,000, and the principal products are sugar and Sea Island cotton, a fine product which is said to have originated in Barbados but now comes especially from Antigua. Montserrat exports lime-juice, and other islands, pineapples, coconuts and minor produce.

THE WINDWARD ISLANDS

The Windward group comprises St. Lucia, St. Vincent, Dominica and Grenada, together with the islets of the Grenadines. All four islands were first settled in the seventeenth century by the English, who had to contend with the fierce Caribs, but St. Lucia and Grenada were for various periods in the possession of the French, with the result that a French patois still prevails amongst their peasantry, although English is spoken throughout the islands. The total area is about 550 square miles and the population is well over 200,000.

The whole group is notable for its varied scenic attractions. St. Lucia, St. Vincent and Grenada, which have been called "the three lovelies", are mountainous and volcanic in character, St. Vincent containing the famous crater Soufriere of which there have been several eruptions. Grenada is known as "the spice island of the West", its chief products being spices and cocoa. St. Lucia has a more varied crop, the chief export being sugar, which with cotten, arrowroot and other products constitute also the exports of St. Vincent. Dominica is the island of which it has been said that Columbus, wishing to demonstrate its shape to Queen Isabella, crumpled up a sheet of parchment and threw it on the table, but the same might be and is said of other West Indian islands. Certainly Dominica has wonderfully rugged scenery and luxurious vegetation.

The seat of the Windwards Government is at St. Georges, the chief town of Grenada, other small capitals being Castries in St. Lucia, Kingstown in St. Vincent, and Roseau in Dominica. Although like the Leewards the group has one Governor, in this case there is no common or central legislature, each island retaining its separate institutions, being administered by a resident Administrator who is also colonial secretary. The constitution of Grenada dates originally from 1766 but has undergone many changes, being progressively freed from official domination and having now an elected majority. St. Lucia was originally governed in accordance with French law, but much the same course has been adopted in this and the other islands as in Grenada, the Administrators governing locally with a mainly elected legislative council.

It has been more than once suggested that the Leeward and Windward islands should form one group under a central administration, but so far this has not come about, and presumably it must now await the decision as to West Indian federation.

Before describing the Bahamas and Bermuda, which are not formally part of the West Indies group, we must turn to the mainland colonies.

British Honduras

British Honduras, a small coastal country in South America about the size of Wales, was once the seat of the old Maya Indian civilization. As a British settlement it had its origin early in the seventeenth century in the visits of tenacious bands of log-cutters or Baymen who, in spite of repeated Spanish attempts to drive them away, remained in possession, aided by friendly Indians, until 1798, when the last attempt to establish Spanish sovereignty was defeated by them in the battle of St. George's Cay. The whole stormy history of the colony is told in the Archives of British Honduras edited by Sir John Burdon, a former Governor. Its early ill-fortune was repeated in 1931, when Belize, the seaport capital, was visited by a hurricane and tidal wave which caused great damage and loss of life.

The colony has now, however, recovered from past calamities and is making steady progress. It has valuable resources in timber, in chicle, the basis of chewing-gum, and other products, and possibly also in minerals. The population however is only some 70,000, and it has been suggested that it should be opened to European settlement for which the bracing and temperate climate of its highlands renders it eminently suitable. The rich forest resources of the interior, largely in mahogany, are carefully administered under a Forest Trust. Its natural resources are not yet fully known, but the country is capable of great development, and various schemes are being investigated.

British Honduras was once subordinate to Jamaica under a lieutenant-Governor, but since 1884 it has had its own Governor and separate administration. The new constitution which will give it similar representative powers to the other mainland colony in South America, is now under consideration. The adjoining state of Guatemala has put forth a shadowy claim to British Honduras as part of her territory, but does not venture to accept the British offer to submit the claim to the United Nations.

British Guiana

The only British colony on the great continent of South America, British Guiana, is the fabled land of El Dorado, which in the past attracted adventurers of all nationalities in search of its mythical golden treasure and civilization. Gold and diamonds British Guiana does possess, but it is no Eldorado and has become better known for its Demerara sugar and other more humdrum but useful products.

There are three Guianas, British, Dutch, and French, lying between the mouths of the Amazon and Orinoco rivers and bounded by Venezuela and Brazil, but the British colony is the largest of the three and its area of some 90,000 square miles is roughly the size of Great Britain. The territory was first partially settled by the Dutch in 1616 and subsequently by the British in 1650 and was finally ceded to Britain in 1814. Originally there were three separate colonies, Demerara, Berbice and Essequibe, named after the three rivers, and these survive as provinces in the present colony. To its Dutch origin it owed several quaint legal survivals such as the Court of Policy and Combined Court, which were only abolished in 1928, the Roman-Dutch law also surviving until 1917.

The total population is around 450,000, of whom the bulk are negroes and East Indians in about equal proportions, although the latter are growing faster. Most of the population is to be found in the coastal belt, the interior being only sparsely inhabited. The capital is Georgetown on the coast and the only other town of importance is New Amsterdam which (unlike New York) has retained its original name. The chief products are sugar and rice, but it also has a growing gold and diamond industry, and a great wealth of timber, especially the famous

Demerara greenheart, as well as coconuts, coffee, rubber and other tropical products.

The country's chief difficulty in the past has been lack of communications with the interior, but this is gradually being overcome. Rail, road, and river steamer services operate in coastal districts, but the rivers are not navigable very far inland owing to cataracts and waterfalls. On the Potare river is the Kaietur Fall, one of the greatest waterfalls in the world and an increasing attraction to tourists and this can be reached both by motor-road and by air services which also serve some of the mines in the interior. More roads are now being driven through the heart of the country and other developments undertaken with the aid of the Colonial Development Fund.

By virtue of its geographical position, British Guiana has been called "the gateway to South America", and undoubtedly when the interior has been opened up and its own great resources more fully developed, a prosperous economic future should lie before British Guiana. It is indeed the natural gateway to Brazil and the immense basin of the Amazon, which will doubtless one day be fully developed. With good sea, air and road communications, it is a key to the great South American continent, and moreover has rich resources of its own, besides great hydro-electric potentialities, only awaiting capital development. An Anglo-American commission reported strongly in 1939 in favour of European immigration and investment, and such a settlement would bring a much-needed influx of population, energy and capital enterprise.

The constitution has been progressively liberalized until now it is based upon adult suffrage and a mainly elected legislature, with responsible Ministers in charge of public business, but just as this was being inaugurated early in 1954, the leaders of the largest political party were accused of subversive political activities, and the constitution had to be suspended pending the report of a special Commission, but this is likely to prove only a temporary check to the country's political progress, since the intention remains to bring about a large measure of self-government as soon as better counsels prevail. A great development scheme for the whole country has recently been recommended by the World Bank and is being initiated.

Both the mainland colonies have so far sent only observers to the West Indian Federation conferences, but their resources and opportunities are undoubtedly needed for a balanced and stable economy, and full co-operation in this respect, especially as they are under-populated, should prove of mutual benefit.

The Bahamas

Although not officially forming part of the British West Indies, this chain of coral islands, the most northerly of the Caribbean archipelago, are for all practical purposes a West Indian group. They include the land first discovered by Columbus in 1492, namely San Salvador or Watling's island. The principal islands besides are New Providence (containing the capital of the group, Nassau), Eleuthera, Grand Bahama, Abaco, Cat and Long islands, Exuma, Andros, Acklins island and Inague. Some score or so of the islands are inhabited and the total area is about 4,500 square miles. The largest is Andros, 100 miles long by about 20 miles in breadth, but the most populous is New Providence, which is also near the centre of the group. The total population is about 75,000.

In the early seventeenth century, the Bahamas were well known to the settlers of Bermuda, and in 1649 the Company of Eleutherian Adventurers was formed in London for the colonization and development of the islands. By 1670 the colonists had organized a form of government including an elective House of Assembly which has survived, though the settlements were sacked by Spaniards and French on various occasions and for a time became the resort of pirates. In 1717 however, the government was resumed by the Crown, its possession being finally confirmed to Great Britain in 1783. After the American revolution, a number of loyalists settled in the islands and the mace formerly used in the South Carolina legislature is still in the Nassau House of Assembly. The present legislature is partly nominated and partly elected, but the trend here as elsewhere is towards giving greater responsibility to the elected element.

The chief industry is sponge fishing, in which hundreds of

small vessels are engaged; but other industries are being developed. Turtles are another notable export. Nassau, the capital, is a fine city and is visited annually by large numbers of Americans and Canadians as well as British, for whom palatial hotels and other tourist attractions are provided. During the reign of prohibition in the United States, Nassau grew rich on the revenue of liquor landed there, and was able to undertake a number of public works on the proceeds, including a new harbour.

BERMUDA

We now go five or six hundred miles north to Shakespeare's "still-vex'd Bermoothes" which, though no part of the West Indies, for some purposes consults with them. Bermuda really consists of a group of many islets and coral reefs, of which however the total area is only some 20 square miles, lying in a concentric ring and connected by roads, bridges and causeways with the main island on which is situated the capital, Hamilton. The islands were discovered in 1515 by a Spaniard, Juan Bermudez, after whom they are named, although they were formerly also called Somers islands, after Admiral Sir George Somers, who formed the first settlement here in 1609.

The islands were first granted by James I to the Virginia Company, which later sold them to the Somers Island or Bermuda Company. A form of representative government was introduced in 1620 but the company's charter was annulled in 1684, when the Crown colony type of government was inaugurated, but the present legislature consists mainly of elected members, and asserting a continuous history from 1620, it claims to be the second oldest parliament in the Commonwealth.

The tourist industry is the main interest of the colony, it being a favourite holiday resort for Americans, Canadians, British and others, especially in the winter, owing to its mild and salubrious climate. It is well served by modern liners and airways, and is equipped with many fine hotels and other attractions. Its sheltered harbours alive with yachting and other craft, its coral islets joined by bridges, set in a blue sea and sky apparently but little "vex'd", Bermuda is a picturesque place. Its houses are beautifully built of soft local stone and its roads of coral limestone are bright and clean. Formerly motor traffic was not allowed, but is now admitted under restrictions. Apart from the tourist traffic, Bermuda grows flowers and vegetables for the American and Canadian markets; the lily fields of Bermuda are a characteristic sight.

Bermuda is a naval station on a small scale and is also the site of an American leased base. It has been found convenient for Anglo-American political conferences. The resident population is some 40,000, about half of whom are white, mainly of English stock, but these are largely augmented by the tourist influx.

Leaving aside Bermuda, all the West Indian islands and mainland colonies are separated by wide stretches of sea and have suffered in the past, and even do to some extent still, from paucity of intercommunication. This isolation has conduced to the growth of "island mentality" and local patriotism, and has so far militated against any form of closer union or federation. But communications of all kinds are now steadily improving and much connective tissue is being built up. The West Indian Conference, established in 1926, was designed to meet alternately in London and the West Indies, to discuss matters concerning agriculture, education, public service, defence, trade and other subjects, and to make recommendations to the Secretary of State and the West Indian Governments. Intercolonial conferences have also been held from time to time to deal with specific subjects, such as customs, trade, etc., and both Bermuda and the mainland colonies have participated in these meetings. As already noted, the Imperial College of Tropical Agriculture in Trinidad serves the West Indies generally and other colonial territories. West Indian interests at home are looked after by the West India Committee, a voluntary body established prior to 1750 and incorporated by Royal Charter in 1904, to promote the agriculture, industries and trade of the West Indies.

In a period of economic depression, a Royal Commission

was appointed in 1938 under the chairmanship of Lord Moyne to consider the needs of the West Indies. The Commission reported in 1940, making a series of drastic recommendations upon which the British Government made a beginning even during the war. A special West Indian Welfare Fund was set up with an annual grant from the Imperial Exchequer of £1,000,000 for twenty years, the fund to be administered by a Comptroller independent of the local governments. Detailed recommendations were made for the improvement of education, public health and housing, the setting up of a trades union for other social services. The report also recommended more intensive use of land, increased production of food for home consumption, further agricultural research, the appointment of an Inspector-General of Agriculture for the West Indies, the improvement of communications and many other reforms. It is now possible to record that very great progress has been made in all these fields and the economic position of the region has steadily improved, although, despite the growth of secondary industries, the economic prosperity of the West Indies will long depend upon the export of their sugar and natural products to British and other markets.

In the political sphere, the Royal Commission recommended federation for the West Indies, and as a preparatory measure the unification of services, extension of the franchise and so forth. Much of this has already been accomplished and the goal is now very much nearer. In 1945 an Anglo-American Caribbean Commission was set up to promote and co-ordinate the social welfare and economic development of both British and American territories in the West Indies, and this proved so successful that the Commission was later enlarged to include the French and Dutch islands and became the Caribbean Commission.

With the improvement of communications and of economic conditions, and the growth of political consciousness and education, there is a much wider horizon in the West Indies today than in the past, and the coming of a West Indian Dominion in the Commonwealth seems only a question of time if only because no single unit (and this includes the mainland colonies) is strong enough to stand on its own feet. Meanwhile, currency, customs and economic agreements and the unification of common services proceed apace.

We turn now to the Atlantic island groups.

St. Helena and Ascension

St. Helena and its sister island of Ascension are situated in the South Atlantic about midway between the South American and African continents, and Tristan da Cunha lies farther south. St. Helena's importance lies far in the past before the days of steam navigation and the Suez Canal. The islands were discovered originally by the Portuguese, but no permanent settlement was founded until the East India Company took possession in 1659. In those days of sail and the Cape route, St. Helena was very conveniently situated on the trade route to India and thousands of ships called there annually to take in fresh provisions and to refill. This was indeed the foundation of the island's prosperity, and a great trade sprang up in the supply of cattle, fruit, vegetables and other provisions in the days before refrigeration. Negroes were brought there to work the plantations and some of their descendants are still there. Modern changes however brought a steady decline in St. Helena's prosperity until it and the sister island of Ascension were chiefly useful only as coaling and cable stations.

St. Helena filled another function in history when it became the place of internment and death of Napoleon, during which period a large garrison was kept in the island. The ex-Emperor lived at Longwood, three or four miles from Jamestown, the capital, and the rather sorry story of those years is fully told in historical annals. He was buried there in May 1821 until the transfer of the remains to Paris in 1840. The house and estate were later presented to the French nation. Other exiles later sojourned in the island; Dinizulu and other Zulu chiefs, and during the South African war, Cronje and other Boer generals and officers.

The present population is some 5,000 souls of very mixed racial origins, chiefly concentrated at and around Jamestown, a quaint and pleasant little town of very English aspect at the seaward mouth of a valley. The climate is equable and healthy, cattle and sheep, and vegetable and other crops thrive, lace-making is carried on, and a phormium flax industry has been established. Housing and other improvements have been carried out with aid from the Colonial Development Fund.

Ascension is entirely occupied by the Cable and Wireless station staff and their dependents and servants from St. Helena, the total population being about 200.

Tristan da Cunha claimed in the past at least to be the "world's loneliest isle", although Pitcairn in the Western Pacific is in a sense a rival claimant. It really consists of a small group of barren volcanic rocks in the South Atlantic some 2,000 miles from Cape Town. The group comprises Tristan itself, Inaccessible, Nightingale and Goughs islands, but only the main island is inhabited. Like Ascension, it is a dependency of St. Helena.

Tristan was named after the Portuguese admiral who discovered the islands in 1506. There was no permanent settlement until 1816, when Britain took possession and garrisoned the island for a short while. On the withdrawal of the garrison, William Glass, an artillery corporal, and his wife with several ex-naval men elected to remain, and this small band being joined by shipwrecked sailors and getting wives from St. Helena, were the founders of the present community, which now numbers some 270. Cattle was kept, potatoes (the staple food) and some fruits were grown and fish was caught, and on this simple basis the islanders lived, being dependent for every other necessity upon rare ships' visits. They clung to their inhospitable home despite several offers by the Union Government in the past to settle them in South Africa, and in time a London fund was established to help tide them over occasional difficulties and to send them some of the more elementary amenities of civilization. Their spiritual needs were looked after by a pastor sent out by the Society for the Propagation of the Gospel, and he with some leading inhabitants became responsible for the primitive community in the civil sphere also.

In the Second World War, however, it became necessary to establish a naval and wireless station on Tristan and this ended its isolation and brought many unaccustomed amenities and some problems, as the community had become somewhat unduly dependent on outside aid. A Tristan Development Company has been set up, which has introduced an organized fishing industry, especially for crawfish which has assured markets, and the people are raising their standards of life. An Administrator has been sent to take charge of the little community with the assistance of the pastor and a small committee of the leading inhabitants.

The Falkland Islands

Before the cutting of the Panama Canal, when all vessels had to double Cape Horn, the Falklands group were much more important than they are today. With their outlying dependencies, they stretch from the toe of South America to the Antarctic circle and the South Pole. As the Antarctic is opened up, they may regain through these dependencies some of their earlier importance.

The main islands are East and West Falkland separated by Falkland Sound and lying about 480 miles north-east of Cape Horn and about 1,000 miles south of Monte Video. There are two groups of dependencies, the first comprising the island of South Georgia with the South Orkney and South Sandwich groups, and the second consisting of the South Shetlands with Grahamland which is part of the Antarctic continent. They derive their chief importance today from the sheep-rearing industry of the Falklands, and the largest whaling industry in the world, centred mainly in the dependencies, especially in South Georgia.

All the islands and Grahamland were discovered by English navigators and explorers, the Falklands themselves first at the end of the sixteenth century, the dependencies in the eighteenth and nineteenth centuries. French and Spanish settlements were later attempted, and the Republic of Buenos Aires claimed the islands in 1820, but all were driven out by 1831, and two years later effective occupation of the islands was resumed by the British Government and has continued ever since. A propagandists' claim to the islands is maintained by Argentina, but is not seriously regarded.

The islands are bare, stony and rugged, but for the hardy islanders, who are largely of Scottish descent, the climate is healthy and the extensive boglands are well suited to rearing sheep, the principal industry, wool, tallow, hides and skins being the chief exports. Meat is cheap and penguin eggs plentiful, but most foodstuffs have to be imported.

The population, which numbers only some 3,000 for the whole group, is mainly concentrated in East Falkland and about half live in the little capital of Port Stanley. There are many good harbours but few roads, and transport is mainly by sea and on horseback, and latterly also by air, the Government having instituted a regular air service. High winds prevail all the year round, which makes it difficult to grow any crops unless they are well protected. The Governor is assisted by a small executive and legislative council, with a majority of elected members.

In the First World War, the Falklands were the scene of a naval battle when a German squadron under Admiral Graf von Spee was caught off Port Stanley by fast battleships despatched from England under Admiral Sturdee and sunk, comparing somewhat with the battle of the River Plate in the Second World War.

The great modern whaling industry which has grown up in the Falklands has its centre in South Georgia and employs both British and Scandinavian seamen. Besides the whaling industry, which has its own factories here, sealing is also undertaken and considerable quantities of seal oil are exported. Whaling research is actively supported by the Falkland Islands Government, which has fitted out several ships for the purpose and for marine surveying and research generally. Among the ships operating in these waters have been the *Discovery*, Captain Scott's ship now at home, *Discovery II*, the *William Scoresby* and the *John Biscoe*. South Georgia is the grave of the Antarctic explorer, Sir Ernest Shackleton, who died in these latitudes in January 1922. What the future exploitation of the Antarctic, in which several nations are interested, will bring to the Falklands colony, remains yet to be seen.

CARIBBEAN AND ATLANTIC COLONIES 43

It is true of these Atlantic islands as it is of similar small island groups in the Pacific that we cannot conceive of their pursuing an independent existence without the support in some form of Britain or the Commonwealth for a very long time to come; and further reference will be made to the future of the smaller colonies in a later part of the book.

CHAPTER IV

THE AFRICAN CONTINENT

THE continent of Africa contains over 80 per cent of all British colonial territories and their future offers some of the profoundest problems which confront us in the colonial sphere. But not only is that future important in itself; it is inescapeably part of the greater problem which is posed by the future of Africa as a whole.

The African continent occupies between one-sixth and one-fifth of the land surface of the globe and in many ways it is the most backward of the continents. In dealing with it here, we are concerned only with Africa south of the Sahara; the countries of the northern littoral may be considered rather as forming part of the Mediterranean basin. Egypt in this sense is not an African power, nor is for example Algeria, which is administered as part of France. The great desert of the Sahara forms a natural barrier between the Mediterranean countries of North Africa and the essentially African scene. Whether this will always be the case is another matter. The Sahara was not always the desert it is today, and although it is still advancing and threatening countries to the south, it can be conquered by man, its boundaries pushed back and its nature transformed.

For the present, however, we confine our attention to the vast territories south of the Sahara covered by Lord Hailey's great *African Survey*, which with later reports and other surveys is likely to form the basis of future development. Africa may be said to have had a "raw deal" from nature, which largely accounts for the later emergence of the "Dark Continent". The soil is in many areas deficient in elements of fertility, which has led to shifting cultivation with consequent erosion and other attendant evils. Many pests and diseases are widely prevalent; the locust and the tsetse-fly, to name only two, do not respect political boundaries. Tropic heat and drought, malnutrition, disease and low vitality have long plagued its peoples, who have suffered not only from their own internecine tribal warfare but from the exploitation of others, Arab and European alike, in the long prevalence of slavery and later of arbitrary political division.

The worst however is past. European exploitation, in the broader sense of the word, has also brought many benefits. Slavery was abolished by the British, internal warfare was suppressed, a large measure of law and order introduced, the continent has been opened up in every direction, and great progress has been made with agriculture, health, education, economic and political development. A beginning has been made in tackling the problems of soil erosion and deforestation and combating malaria, leprosy, the locust and the tsetse-fly and other pests and diseases. Railways, roads and harbours have been built, rivers and lakes navigated, airways developed, public works and social services installed, mineral resources exploited and many new crops and industries introduced. It is a vastly different Africa today from what it was even a half-century ago, and its peoples have shown that given favourable conditions, they are as apt and intelligent as any other race of mankind. Certainly there is no foundation for any theory of "natural inferiority" of the African once his heavy natural handicaps are removed.

In the latter half of the last century, tropical Africa was the scene of a scramble by the European powers, in which the British Government, as distinct from some of its more enterprizing citizens took a belated and reluctant part. As a result, the greater part of the continent was more or less arbitrarily parcelled out between them, natural or racial divisions being little regarded in the process, and in some cases even tribal boundaries ignored. Africa today is consequently a political patchwork in which many of the territories have largely an artificial structure corresponding to no natural boundaries. Nevertheless, for good or ill, the tribal stage is passing in Africa as it did long ago in Europe, and a new nationalism is growing up in some of these countries stimulated by this very process of Westernization and increasing contacts with the world at large. In South Africa of course the Europeans, both

British and Dutch, came centuries ago, even before the Bantu penetrated southwards.

The total population is estimated at around 165,000,000; but there are no reliable data. Indeed all kinds of surveys and vital statistics are badly needed, and all that can be said is that with settled and improved conditions, the population is now steadily growing. Compared with the size of the continent, that is not a large number; in fact, except Australia, Africa has the lowest density of population in relation to area of any continent. Britain and the Union of South Africa between them are responsible for a large part of this area and population, and as we have seen in the introduction, Britain's responsibilities might have been even greater. France comes next with vast territories in French West and Equatorial Africa, and the other European powers concerned are Belgium, for the Congo, and Portugal for Angola and Mozambique. Although their policies and methods vary greatly, co-operation, as we shall see later, is steadily growing between these powers in matters affecting Africa. The sole Spanish foothold is the backward Rio de Oro.

The oldest British settlements in Africa were those on the West Coast, where English traders had been active since the sixteenth century, and in the scramble for Africa, Britain might have acquired much more territory in this region, possibly linking the Gold Coast and Nigeria and stretching across to the Sudan, were it not for her reluctance to undertake further responsibilities; and it was chiefly due to the persistence of men like Sir George Goldie and later Lord Lugard, apart from the pressure of events, that the present territories were acquired. Even the Congo was first offered to Britain, as well as parts of what is now French Equatorial Africa. Indeed, that remarkable woman, Mary Kingsley, to whom West Africa owes so much, used to say that for forty years after Waterloo the whole of West Africa from the Gambia to the Congo was Britain's if she had chosen to take it. Although this may seem today rank imperialism, unfortunately there was no question of West Africa being left to itself. Other powers stepped in and seized what Britain refused, and it is vain to speculate now what otherwise might have been the subsequent history of this great region of Africa.

From north to south and passing round the "bulge" of Africa, the four present British territories are the Gambia, Sierra Leone, the Gold Coast and Nigeria.

The Gambia

The colony and protectorate of the Gambia is the smallest of our African territories, being a mere riverain strip extending from St. Mary's Island at the mouth to some 250 miles upstream on both banks of the river, a total area of a little over 4,000 square miles. Bathurst, the seat of government, is situated on St. Mary's island. The total population is a little over 250,000.

The Gambia was first discovered by the Portuguese, but the English were the first to trade, forming a succession of companies from 1588 to 1816. In 1821 the settlement was annexed to Sierra Leone and administered by a Lieutenant-Governor, but in 1843 it was created a separate colony with a Governor and executive and legislative councils on the usual Crown colony model. For a time it formed part of the government of the West African Settlements, but reverted to separate administration in 1888. There is now an unofficial majority on the Council and certain of the unofficial members are appointed to the executive without portfolio to advise on government affairs.

The Gambia is little more than a long wedge driven into French Senegal, but it has a character of its own. The great highway is of course the Gambia river which is navigable for nearly 300 miles from its mouth, and the protectorate extends to a depth of six miles on either bank. The wealth of the Gambia is based on groundnuts, which are the chief crop, although hides and palm kernels are also exported, and other products are grown for local consumption. An ambitious project for poultry rearing on a large scale sponsored by the Colonial Development Corporation unfortunately failed, but great attention is now being given to improving the farms to grow more food, especially rice. Compared with the other West

African colonies, the Gambia has received little attention and its future as a separate economic entity is dubious.

Sierra Leone

Sierra Leone lies on the coast between the republic of Liberia and French Guinea and was originally named by the Portuguese from the fancied resemblance of its coastal mountain to the form of a lion. It had its origin as a British colony in the movement for the abolition of the slave trade, whence its capital, Freetown, derives its name. In the central square was long to be seen the tree at the foot of which slaves' shackles were struck off.

The colony and protectorate comprise an area of about 28,000 square miles, with a population of some 2,000,000. It was first settled in 1785 and grew by successive cessions of territory by native chiefs; in 1896 a protectorate was declared over the hinterland. For some time the colony was administered as a part of the West African Settlements with the Gold Coast and Lagos, and when these were separated, still in conjunction with the Gambia, which was finally separated from Sierra Leone in 1888. The population is almost entirely African and especially in Freetown and the coastal districts, it is among the most sophisticated on the West Coast.

The Executive and Legislative councils now have elected majorities and unofficial members of the Executive council act as Ministers in charge of groups of departments. The principal exports are palm kernels and palm oil, cocoa, ginger and other natural products, but there has also been a considerable development of iron ore for export from the Marampa mines. The Government railway was the first to be constructed in West Africa, roads have been built throughout the country and the deep-water quays at Freetown have berths for the largest ships. Minor industries and the processing of products are also being encouraged under development schemes. Fourah Bay College is affiliated to Durham University at home and forms part of the scheme for university training in West Africa.

The Gold Coast

The second largest of the British colonies in West Africa and politically the most advanced is somewhat misleadingly named. Although gold was the original attraction and is still an important export, the mainstay of the country's economy today is cocoa, of which the Gold Coast provides one-third of the world's total supply. With Ashanti, the Northern Territories and British Togoland, it covers an area of about 92,000 square miles, approximately equal to Great Britain, and has a population of over 4,500,000.

The first Europeans to settle on the Gold Coast were the Portuguese, who arrived in 1471 and built the castle at Elmina in 1482. They were followed in 1595 by the Dutch, who succeeded to all the Portuguese possessions on the coast in 1642. The British and the Danes followed, the latter making their only appearance in Africa and leaving Christianborg Castle, now the Governor's official residence, as their sole relic. The British, whose headquarters were then at Cape Coast Castle, finally displaced the others after an internecine struggle.

The main divisions of the country are the Gold Coast proper in the south, Ashanti to the north, and farther north still the Northern Territories, with on the east a strip of Togoland under British mandate, the larger part of Togoland being under French mandate. This roughly oblong territory with a coast-line of about 340 miles lies between the French Ivory Coast on the west and French Togoland on the east, which with Dahomey divides it from Nigeria.

Ashanti has a stormy history. In the coastal regions, the people, mostly immigrants, developed over long years into small autonomous units under European protection and without tribal tradition, but in the interior, tribal organization, practically untouched by European influences, was strong, and the most highly organized was the Ashanti federation which began to harry its neighbours, especially the coastal peoples, and to demand a greater share in trade. Continuous local conflicts led to the intervention of the British and the bellicose spirit of King Prempeh, whose centre was at Kumasi, brought about the Ashanti campaigns, and finally led to the annexation of

Ashanti in 1901 and the deposition of Prempeh. He went into exile but was allowed to return in 1924. Ten years later the Ashanti Confederation was restored, and in 1935 Prempeh's successor under the title of Prempeh II was proclaimed Asantehene or paramount ruler of the Ashanti tribes. The famous Golden Stool, the traditional abiding place of the soul of the Ashanti people, was at the same time restored. Since then, Ashanti has always enjoyed considerable local autonomy under its native administration and has made substantial economic and social progress, the once bloodstained capital of Kumasi being now a progressive modern city with up-to-date amenities under its own municipality.

The Northern Territories, which came under British influence in 1897, have also made great strides economically and in the sphere of native administration, where direct taxation was introduced to aid local treasuries, which are well managed. British Togoland is divided into north and south districts for administrative purposes with the adjoining Gold Coast territories.

In recent years, great political progress has been made in the Gold Coast and the colony (which some wish to call by the African name of Ghana) is now well advanced on the road to self-government. It is indeed held up as a pattern and ideal by other less advanced African communities, whilst those who fear and distrust African political progress (especially in South Africa) regard it as a warning and portent. The British Government has pursued a courageous and enlightened policy which has so far on the whole been justified by results and by the sense of responsibility shown by the new administration, though the country still has a testing time ahead.

Acting on the Cousey Report (presided over by an African judge) and in pursuance of its general colonial policy, the Government introduced adult suffrage combined with the operation of electoral colleges in the native authority areas and for the large municipalities, and the first elections under the new constitution were ably organized and carried out peacefully in 1951, the result being a sweeping victory for the Convention People's Party under its leader, Dr. Nkrumah. Since then further advances have been made and Dr. Nkrumah became Prime Minister at the head of a responsible Cabinet of Ministers. In accord with the Home Government, he later invited suggestions from representative opinion throughout the country with a view to achieving complete self-government at an early date. A Public Service Commission has been in operation, the civil service has been reorganized and arrangements made for progressive Africanization. The colony is divided into four Regions under Chief Regional Officers, and new Government buildings have been completed at Accra. Local government has been strengthened and progress is being made in many spheres. There is need for a stronger and more united opposition to the principal party in parliament, but broadly speaking the country is entering on its new era under generally favourable auspices.

Economic progress has been steady. Although the principal product, cocoa, was attacked by swollen shoot disease, this was countered by a determined cutting-out policy, and cocoa represents two-thirds of the total exports. It is conservatively and wisely controlled by the Cocoa Marketing Board, which accumulates a valuable reserve fund. Besides gold and diamonds and other mineral exports, timber is another very valuable product. The country possesses a great forest area of varied timber, especially mahogany. The "closed forest" region, in which cocoa farming also prevails, has a permanently protected area of 7,000 square miles, and it has been estimated that there is an annual exportable surplus of over 5,000,000 cubic feet of merchantable timber of all kinds. The humid closed forest area is necessary to the continuance of the cocoa industry as a protection from arid conditions. Palm oil and kernels, kola nuts, copra and rubber also figure among the exports.

The country possesses valuable deposits of bauxite and manganese, and a great project which is going forward is the Volta River scheme for hydro-electric power based on an aluminium industry. Tema harbour is being constructed on the coast with United Kingdom assistance and further development schemes are in prospect.

The country has owed much to wise Governors in the past, like Sir Gordon Guggisberg, and to prominent Africans such as Dr. Aggrey. At the apex of the educational system stands that fine institution, Achimota College, which is providing increasing numbers of African men and women with education up to university standard in their own country, and with similar institutions at Ibadan in Nigeria and Fourah Bay in Sierra Leone, the foundations are laid for a University of West Africa. There is a College of Technology at Kumasi and both primary and secondary education with training facilities for teachers, besides medical, public health and other social services, are growing apace throughout the country.

The Government railway system comprises well over 500 miles of line and is still extending; there is a fine modern harbour at Takoradi, many hundreds of miles of motor roads and well developed public services of all kinds. The Gold Coast Regiment of the West African Frontier Force has a fine soldierly tradition. The country has undoubtedly a great future, even considered apart from the rest of West Africa.

NIGERIA

This is by far the largest of the West African colonies and is indeed in many ways the greatest of British African territories, for although Tanganyika is very slightly larger in area, it has only a quarter of the population. Nigeria covers an area of nearly 373,000 square miles, that is to say, roughly four times the size of the United Kingdom, and has a population of over 30,000,000 still steadily growing. The country is far too little known in Britain or for that matter in the rest of the world. It may be said to offer one of many examples of arbitrary political division in Africa, for the country and especially its peoples are so diverse that, in the approach to self-government, only a federal constitution has been found workable, although despite all differences there is already a growth of Nigerian national consciousness.

Nigeria's history is bound up with British trading posts established at the mouths of the great Niger river in the Gulf of Guinea since the seventeenth century, with explorations of the river by Mungo Park, the Lander brothers, McGregor Laird and other travellers, and especially with the formation of the Royal Niger Company by Sir George Goldie and the subsequent settlement of the country by Lord Lugard. Despite many failures and constant hostilities, British traders persisted in their efforts to open up the interior to trade, and eventually the various trading interests were amalgamated by Sir George Goldie into what became the Royal Niger Company, which obtained its charter in 1886. The company was energetic in extending its trading posts, consolidating the organization, concluding treaties with native chiefs and tribes, vigilantly watching and outflanking French and German encroachments, and finally in fighting the great Fulani power centred at Sokoto. These activities first saw the emergence of Captain (later Lord) Lugard, who started in the service of the Company and afterwards became Commissioner and Commandant of the West African Frontier Force for the British Government, which revoked the Charter of the Company and transferred its rights and powers to the Crown in 1898. Agreements for the delimitation of boundaries were reached with France and Germany (then active in the Cameroons) and the powerful Emirates of the Hausa states in the north and the kingdom of Bornu were finally brought under control with the occupation of Kano and Sokoto in 1903.

Whilst these events were taking place in Northern Nigeria, of which Colonel Lugard had become High Commissioner, British influence was being effectively extended over the south, including the mouth of the Niger and the coastal region known as the Oil Rivers Protectorate, the kingdom of Benin, and Lagos. A treaty was concluded with the King of Benin by Captain (later Sir Henry) Galway in 1892, but as this was ignored and the rule of Benin (which was said to extend from Sierra Leone to the Congo) was accompanied by orgies of human sacrifice, massacre of Europeans and other atrocities, an expedition was finally sent against Benin City, which was found in an indescribable condition, and the king fled and finally died at Calabar in 1914.

The colony of Lagos (now the capital of Nigeria) originated in efforts, ultimately successful, to suppress the slave trade on the Guinea coast. Other expeditions had to be undertaken in various parts of southern Nigeria before law and order could be brought to the turbulent tribes of the region, but eventually all these districts were amalgamated into the colony and protectorate of Southern Nigeria in 1906.

Northern and Southern Nigeria pursued independent courses for some years, since conditions in each differed and still differ) greatly, but eventually in 1914 they were amalgamated and Lord Lugard, who had taken an outstanding part in building up the country, became the first Governor-General. During all this time, despite military operations and the unsettled state of a vast and almost unknown country, development was steadily going on, roads and railways were being built, port works started at Lagos, trade expanded and civil administration established. The Niger Company, until taken over by the Crown, had done remarkable work in opening up the country to peaceful commercial development and laying the foundations of ordered rule. After the First World War, the German Cameroons became, like Togoland, a mandated territory, but as with Togoland, France became responsible for the major portion, only a narrow strip on the west being incorporated in Nigeria.

The principal groups of peoples in Nigeria are the Hausa and Fulani states of the north, well organized in strong Mahommedan emirates with traditions derived from Arab origins, and the more sophisticated but looser Yoruba and Ibo tribes of the south although there are many subdivisions, apart from the pagans of the hills. Lugard, who, as we shall see, had had previous experience in Uganda, found in the powerful emirates of the north inspiration for his system of Indirect Rule, which he introduced in Nigeria. All these states retain their own administrations, courts and treasuries, advised and assisted by British officers, but exercising their own jurisdiction and authority within the framework of the Colonial Government. Their rulers, whose status was fully recognized, played an important part in the development of Nigeria, and as representative institutions were progressively introduced, they took their own place in the constitutional structure of the country.

The general administrative headquarters of Nigeria are at Lagos on the coast, while the northern and southern provincial centres are at Kaduna and Enugu respectively. It was originally hoped to build up a strong centralized government, but in view of the differences between north and south, this has not proved feasible; and the new constitution introduced in 1951, based on adult suffrage, provided for a federal structure. The country is divided into three Regions, Northern, Western and Eastern, apart from Lagos, the federal centre. Each Region has a Lieutenant-Governor and its own Assembly which is represented in the Central Legislature. The Regional assemblies are almost entirely composed of Nigerians elected either directly or through electoral colleges in the case of the emirates and other organized communities. Both in the Central and in the Regional legislatures, there are executive Councils of Ministers formed largely of native Nigerians, and although there have been many party dissensions and manoeuvrings, and regional differences, the country as a whole is gradually settling down to work out a practical solution for the future. The Secretary of State recently presided over conferences both in London and in Nigeria which settled outstanding problems and tried to get the new Constitution on a stable basis with great prospects of future progress. Local government throughout the country has also been strengthened, and native authorities liberalized, chiefs consulting elected councils in their administration.

The actual and potential wealth of the country is considerable. The principal exports are palm oil and kernels, tin, gold, coal, cocoa, mahogany and other timbers, cotton, groundnuts, hides and skins, etc. Nigeria, like Malaya, is an important tin exporter, the principal tin mines being situated on the Bauchi plateau of which the town of Jos is the centre. There are many minor products, apart from a varied and growing home consumption, and bananas are exported from the Cameroons. As in the Gold Coast, marketing boards control some of the principal products.

There is an extensive Government railway system, with its own workshops at Enugu and Eboute Metta, and motor roads traverse the country in all directions. The rivers Niger and Benue are in themselves great natural highways, and air communications are fast developing not only within Nigeria but between it and other African countries and the rest of the world. The principal towns are Ilorin, Jos, Kaduna, Kano, Katsina, Maidugari, Sokoto, Yola, Abeokuta, Benin, Calabar, Enugu, Forcados, Ibadan, Onitsha, Oyo, Port Harcourt and Warri, but the largest is Lagos, the federal capital.

The fine University College established at Ibadan crowns the educational system. Nigeria has been fortunate in its Governors and civil service, and its administration and public services are at a high level. With such diverse peoples, on the whole conservative and cautious but well organized in the north, politically conscious and sophisticated in the south, Nigeria faces a great destiny fraught with many problems, in which Nigerians must play an increasingly decisive part as they advance towards responsible self-government and a leading role in the future of West Africa.

The West African colonies differ from other British territories in Africa in that they are not suitable for white settlement. They have therefore none of the problems of plural communities. In the old days, the West Coast had an evil reputation as "the white man's grave", but this it has long outgrown. The advance of medical and sanitary science, of housing and social conditions, and the coming of many amenities of civilization, as well as changes in personal habits, have rendered the lives of European official and mercantile communities as healthy as it can be under tropical conditions. White women are also now able to live on the Coast and this has naturally made a great difference. But when all is said and done, white people cannot live permanently in West Africa, and in any case land is not allowed to be alienated to Europeans. The future of West Africa therefore lies primarily with the African, although there is still ample scope for European guidance and technical assistance. The present communities should not however forget the debt they owe not only to the great pioneers of the past but also to the obscure and not always reputable traders who laid the foundations of present prosperity and for the most part left their bones on the Coast.

Nigeria and the Gold Coast (or Ghana) are great countries in themselves, quite apart from their relation to West Africa as a whole, and if present developments continue on a stable basis, they can have an assured future in the Commonwealth as independent units, but this is scarcely true of the Gambia or even of Sierra Leone as viable economic units under modern conditions, and with the growth of communications and common interests, it may prove possible in the future to revive under more favourable conditions the federation of British West Africa which was attempted prematurely in the earlier Settlements. Close economic and administrative links already exist between the four colonies, and the West African Governors Conference provides for regular consultation and co-operation: the two larger colonies have a certain measure of responsibility in this connexion.

British West African territories are however embedded in and surrounded by French Union territory, and despite considerable and growing co-operation between the present colonial powers in Africa, their general policy and methods differ in many respects, and Britain is the only power with a declared policy of self-government for its present colonial peoples. This therefore is part of the problem of the future of Africa as a whole to which further reference will be made at the end of this African chapter.

Before turning to other British African territories, brief reference should here be made to the Sudan. This vast country, covering more than 1,000,000 square miles and stretching from the southern border of Egypt to the boundaries of Abyssinia, was never a colony and its complete independence now rests in the hands of its own people, but the story of its rescue from the chaos, depopulation and misrule which overtook it in the days of the Mahdi and its subsequent progress to the prosperous community which it is today is one of which this country primarily has every reason to be proud. Until its achievement of self-government, the Sudan was a condominium of Britain and Egypt (which had itself become an independent kingdom in 1922) but the Sudan Political Service with a British Governor-General at its head was largely British in composition, though Egyptians and, of course, Sudanese were associated with it; and whilst acting under the Foreign Office, its methods and traditions were closely akin to those of the Colonial Service (from which indeed appointments were often made) and its standards were of the highest.

To prepare the people for self-government was consistently the declared objectives of British policy in the Sudan, and the country may be said to owe both its economic and its political advancement very largely to Great Britain, The history of the Sudan must be sought elsewhere, but British capital, administration and the skill of British engineers have transformed the country. Great dams at Assuan, Assiut and Sennar regulate the flow of the Nile and conserve its life-giving waters, the Gezira and other irrigation schemes have brought former arid regions under cultivation, new crops, especially cotton, have been introduced and are now cultivated on a great scale, the lot of the peasant has been much improved, and education, health and public services of all kinds have made substantial strides.

Khartoum is a fine modern, well-planned city situated at the confluence of the Blue and White Niles. It is an ideal site for the capital and is a great meeting-place for traffic by rail, river, road and air. It is directly connected by rail with the well-equipped harbour of Port Sudan on the Red Sea, and has both rail and river connexions with the Mediterranean through Egypt and with all Africa to the south. Moreover it is a great air junction for airliners flying between Cairo and the Cape and also across to West Africa. Already it is possible to fly from London to Khartoum, a distance of over 3,000 miles, in about six and a half hours, and doubtless in future this will be even further reduced. In the Gordon Memorial College at Khartoum and its affiliated schools has been laid the foundation of a University for the Sudan.

The people of the North are much more advanced and sophisticated than those of the South and special provision for the interests of the latter had to be made in the constitution; its success will depend upon co-operation between the two and the wisdom and restraint of Sudanese statesmen and parliament. Since both Egypt and the Sudan are ultimately dependent upon the Nile waters, Egypt's close interest in the Sudan is fully understandable, but there is no reason why an independent Sudan should not maintain close links with both Egypt and the

Commonwealth. In any case, the building up of the Sudan into a nation cannot be omitted from Britain's record in Africa.

Let us now turn to East and Central Africa. These comprise in East Africa, Kenya, Uganda and Tanganyika, with Zanzibar off the coast, and in Central Africa, Northern and Southern Rhodesia and Nyasaland, now joined in the Central African Federation. The remaining British territories in Africa are British Somaliland on the "horn" of Africa, and the High Commission territories of Basutoland, Swaziland and Bechuanaland, embedded in or adjoining the Union of South Africa. Since historically British influence in East Africa began in the Arab sultanate of Zanzibar, whose rule formerly extended over considerable areas of the mainland, it may be appropriate to begin with that now small country.

ZANZIBAR

Zanzibar and Pemba, once the centre of the Zenj empire, are two small islands off the East coast with a total area of 1,020 square miles. It is now a British protectorate. The Zenj empire was founded from Shiraz in Arabia in 975, but was already in decline when the Portuguese conquered the coast early in the sixteenth century. They gave way to the Imams of Muscat in the next century and finally Seyyid Said transferred his capital to Zanzibar in 1832. At this time Arab power in East Africa was so strong that it gave rise to the saying that "if a man plays on the flute in Zanzibar, everybody as far as the lakes dances".

In 1856 the Zanzibar sultanate became independent of Muscat. At this time, British influence was high, largely owing to the excellent work and wise counsel of Sir John Kirk, friend of Livingstone and later consul-general at Zanzibar; but the rivalries of European powers in East Africa were now beginning, and France, Italy and especially Germany, were active on the coast and in the interior, where Karl Peters in particular used unscrupulous methods to advance German interests. Kirk saw clearly what was happening, but the British Government was apathetic and allowed German influence to spread on the mainland until 1890, when an agreement was reached whereby

Germany recognized the British protectorate over Zanzibar and the inclusion of Uganda in the British sphere of influence; but this left a large tract of country in German hands, thus frustrating Rhodes's dream of an "all-red" route from the Cape to Cairo, which had to wait until after the First World War for its realization. Meanwhile, this great tract of country became German East Africa, the corresponding British territory was originally known as Ibea, from the initials of the Imperial British East Africa Company. Their territory was taken over by the Crown in 1895 and became British East Africa, later Kenya, including a coastal strip rented from the Sultan of Zanzibar. In Zanzibar itself British influence became supreme, Sir Lloyd Matthews proving a worthy successor to Sir John Kirk. Steady progress has been made and the country is administered with the advice of the British Resident. Although Arabs are the ruling caste, the bulk of the population consists of Swahilis from the neighbouring mainland.

Zanzibar and Pemba have practically a world monopoly of cloves, which were first introduced by Seyyid Said. The port of Zanzibar is also a busy centre for East African trade and the old city retains many interesting and picturesque relics of an earlier civilization.

KENYA

The former territory of British East Africa took its present name from Mount Kenya, the second highest mountain in Africa, when it became a colony in 1920. It is roughly 225,000 square miles in extent, but was once larger, for in 1924 the province of Jubaland was freely ceded to Italy and in the following year there was an adjustment of the frontier with the adjoining Uganda Protectorate.

Kenya largely owes its present development to the construction of the Kenya and Uganda Railway. This great project was undertaken by the British Government in 1895 to give Uganda, situated 500 miles inland, needed access to the coast. It was not expected that the tropical coastal region would itself be of much value, and the damp sultry heat of Mombasa, the principal port, and of the whole low-lying fever-haunted coastal strip confirmed this view. But as railway construction progressed and the line reached the highlands, a dry bracing climate was found at altitudes ranging from 3,000 to 7,000 feet, which was apparently quite suitable for European settlement. The completion of the line therefore brought in its train a stream of white settlers for the highlands of Kenya, and the movement was actively encouraged by the British Government after the First World War, when many ex-servicemen and others wished to emigrate.

The soil of the highlands was discovered to be eminently suitable for coffee planting, general farming and stock-raising, and as all these activities needed capital investment to be prosecuted on a large scale, the country attracted a class of settlers of whom perhaps Lord Delamere, whose life is a sort of epitome of Kenya history, may serve as a typical example. There were also of course many of more modest means who sought in Kenya a healthy livelihood by hard pioneer work, raising coffee, sisal, maize, livestock, and later exploiting gold and other minerals, and who formed the backbone of the remarkable development of the country. At that time, the White Highlands, as they became known and indeed most of the huge country, was but sparsely inhabited by wandering Masai, Kikuyu and other tribes who did not practise settled cultivation. The settlers were largely of the same class as the officials sent out to administer the country and being accustomed to manage their own affairs, expected similar freedom in their adopted country.

The opportunities of the new country also attracted a large Indian immigration in the form of merchants and traders, clerks, storekeepers and mechanics who came in the wake of the railway, and who stayed to take advantage of the commercial and other developments. The extension of ordered government brought about changes in the habits of the tribes and a steady increase in population, which was further stimulated by wider opportunities of varied employment both on the European farms and in the growing towns, though this led in time to detribalization and other problems.

On the land, increasing pressure necessarily reduced wasteful habits of shifting cultivation, but this gave rise to land grievances, especially among the Kikuyu, who though they formed only about 20 per cent of the native population, were the most articulate and politically conscious. Friction also arose between Africans and the Indian immigrants, although relations have latterly improved and Africans are actually replacing Indians as skilled craftsmen and small traders. Meanwhile the European community, which had done so much to develop the resources of the country, not unnaturally claimed an increasing share in the government of the colony (which like others was originally administered on the Crown colony system with an official majority) and the elected European members, with representatives of the other races, now form the majority in the legislature.

Throughout its comparatively short history, Kenya has unfortunately attracted more than its full share of press and political controversy and not always well-informed criticism at home. Within the limits of an introductory work of this kind, it is impossible to discuss these questions adequately without taking up disproportionate space, and it must therefore suffice to state some of the outstanding facts as briefly as possible and to suggest the need for fuller study, towards which some sources are indicated in the bibliography. But Kenya cannot be studied in isolation from the rest of Africa, some of whose problems will be referred to later.

For a young community Kenya has made remarkable progress, and apart from sound administration, this must in fairness be attributed largely to the pioneer efforts and enterprise of the European community, many of whom have devoted their lives to the country and are bringing up their children there. This community has undoubtedly still a vital and indispensable role to play in the future of Kenya (as indeed in other parts of Africa) but this must be in partnership and co-operation with the other races in the country. Most of the Europeans live at fairly high altitudes and it is not yet certain what effect this may have on future generations.

The population of the country is well over 5,500,000, of whom of course the great bulk are African of various tribes, Europeans numbering some 30,000 and Indians, Arabs and others over 100,000. The legislative council consists at present of a Speaker and fifty-four members with an unofficial majority in which the Europeans predominate over other races, but Africans have been appointed to the Executive and further constitutional progress must certainly provide for increased representation of the other races.

Kenya is suffering from the difficulties inherent in plural communities, and in Africa as elsewhere these can only be solved by mutual co-operation, toleration and good sense. These qualities will not be found lacking in Kenya, despite the outbreak of the Mau Mau rebellion amongst the Kikuyu in 1953, which necessitated military aid from Britain. Though the causes were complex and obscure, there is no question as to the real answer, which is to press on with the land and other reforms proposed by the latest Commission. Earlier commissions had already dealt with land problems and also with questions concerning taxation, finance, customs and closer union between Kenya and other East African territories. It may be that, despite the natural reluctance of the purely African communities of Uganda to form any such association, the ultimate future of East Africa must lie in some such union or federation as already exists in Central Africa. Purely African interests in the individual territories can always be safeguarded in any such association which would certainly be advantageous at least from the economic point of view. There is already a customs union between Kenya and Uganda which is mutually beneficial. The East African Governors Conference with its later development the High Commission controls international services and is concerned with all matters of common interest.

Meanwhile, as soon as it has recovered from internal troubles Kenya can go forward with confidence. Its economy is sound and it has great potentialities for future development. Agriculture, both native and European, is being steadily improved new industries such as pyrethrum have been successfully introduced, the mineral industry is steadily growing in importance and the standard of living is being progressively raised. Though many problems remain to be tackled, education, health and the public services are advancing. Nairobi is a fine modern city, though native housing is still a civic problem; in Mombasa and Kilindini on the coast Kenya possesses first-rate port facilities, and its rail, road and air communications are steadily improving. In the air, it not only has good local services, but is on the direct trans-African air route from north to south, besides being connected with West Africa through Khartoum.

Kenya's future depends upon Kenyans of all races working together. A Council of Ministers representative of Europeans, Africans and Indians has already been set up experimentally and may lead to further political development when the emergency is over.

UGANDA

Unlike her eastern neighbour Kenya, and like the West African colonies, the Uganda protectorate is entirely an African territory. The country is associated not only with the explorations of Speke and Grant, the former of whom discovered the source of the Nile in Victoria Nyanza, but also with the journeys of Dr. Livingstone. The Nile issues from the Victoria Nyanza at the Ripon Falls, flows through other lakes and into the Sudan at Nimule: the source of the Blue Nile is in Abyssinia at Lake Tana, so that these two countries ultimately control the Nile waters. The area of the protectorate is some 94,000 square miles, including the great lakes, and the total population is about 5,250,000. The climate is tropical and unsuited for white settlement.

The great possibilities of the country were first seen by Captain (later Lord) Lugard, then acting for the British East Africa Company, but it was at that time the scene of constant strife and was nearly abandoned by the British before a protectorate was eventually proclaimed in 1894, and even then the rulers of the Baganda people were engaged in continuous warfare with the neighbouring tribes. In 1897 Sir Harry Johnston was sent out as special commissioner, and since then its record has been one of peaceful progress and economic prosperity.

Before the advent of the Kenya and Uganda Railway, the country was cut off from the sea, but with good rail, road and air connexions it has been opened up to trade. The chief crop grown and the main source of its wealth is cotton, the industry being largely in native hands. Trade also flows through the great lakes and the Nile to Egypt and the Mediterranean. The protectorate is divided into four provinces of which the most important is the kingdom of Buganda. The garden city of Entebbe is the legislative centre, but the chief commercial towns are Kampala and Jinja, the latter the site of the great Owen Falls hydro-electric project on the Nile.

The Baganda people are the most progressive in the country and they have always had a settled government under their king, the Kabaka, assisted by his own ministers and the council or Lukiko. It was indeed the existence and efficient functioning of this government that first led Lugard to his conception of Indirect Rule which he later applied on a greater scale in Nigeria. Reforms were initiated by the Protectorate Government in the composition of the central legislative council, and in the Buganda Lukiko which were resisted by the Kabaka Mutesa II and led to his deposition in 1954 and the appointment of regents. The Buganda kingdom has always been jealous of its unique position compared with the other provinces and a fear that this might be affected by changes in Uganda or in East Africa led to a separatist movement which however was contrary to the agreement of 1900 with the British Government and would have jeopardized the stability of the whole country. Firm assurances have however been given that nothing would be allowed to affect the local autonomy of Buganda, but there appears to be need that the government should become more representative of the Buganda people. There now seems to be good prospect of the reforms being put through with the help and advice of Sir Keith Hancock, who undertook a special mission.

The people as a whole are prosperous and industrious. There are over 2,000,000 acres under cotton, which forms 80 per cent of the value of all exports, coffee, tobacco and oilseeds being amongst the others. Cotton growers have now been set up under native control. The country has an excellent railway and road system, airports, river and lake navigation, and will further benefit by the development of hydro-electric power at Owen Falls and the Uganda Development Corporation is actively promoting other schemes. Great strides have been made in medical, social and educational work, and at Makerere near Kampala, Uganda possesses the nucleus of a future university for East Africa.

TANGANYIKA

The largest British territory in East Africa, 374,000 square miles in extent, differs in status from the others in being a mandate, but it is administered in precisely the same way as other colonial territories, the only difference being that an annual report on its progress is submitted to the Trusteeship Council of the United Nations, Great Britain being the first voluntarily to adopt this arrangement in respect of her mandated territories. Tanganyika is usually considered to be identical with the former German East Africa, but this is not strictly accurate, for the most populous and fertile portion, the Ruanda-Urundi district, was mandated to Belgium and joined with the Belgian Congo, and the Rovuma river district went to Portugal.

The name Tanganyika derives from the long lake on the western border, meaning "great meeting of the waters". Lakes Nyasa and Victoria also form part of the boundaries, and the country includes the highest mountain in Africa, Mount Kilima Njaro, 19,750 feet in height. The greater part of the interior is occupied by an elevated plateau, which like the similar region in Kenya was found suitable for white settlement originally by Germans. The European population however numbers less than 20,000 and Asians about 80,000 out of a total of nearly 8,000,000 Africans largely of mixed Bantu stock.

The capital is Dar-es-Salaam on the coast below Zanzibar, and other towns include Tanga, also on the coast opposite Pemba, Usambari, Moshi, Tabora Mwanza on Lake Victoria, and Ujiji on Lake Tanganyika, where Stanley met Livingstone. The East African campaign in the First World War was fought over this country.

The railway system connects with that of Kenya and with the steamers on the great lakes. Amongst the principal exports are sisal, tea, coffee, maize, tobacco, and mineral products and there are large timber reserves. The natural resources of Tanganyika have indeed barely yet been exploited and there is considerable scope for development, which is proceeding after a false start when an ambitious scheme for the cultivation of groundnuts on a large scale failed for lack of adequate preparation.

Local government is being strengthened throughout the country, and constitutional developments are also proceeding, and as conditions here differ from those in Kenya, these are based on equal representation of the three races on the unofficial side of the new legislative council which assumes office in 1956.

Throughout East Africa, the native peoples are far less advanced than those in West Africa, and much remains yet to be done in the economic, social and political spheres before they can compare, except possibly in Buganda, with the West Africans. Moreover, the problem is here complicated by the existence in two territories of white settlement, but self-government remains the objective of British colonial policy, and this is the end which must ultimately be achieved in one form or another by its various peoples. Whether it will be possible to form some kind of federal association between the several East African territories whilst protecting local interests, and even between them and Central Africa, only the future can decide.

Central African Federation

The three territories of Southern Rhodesia, Northern Rhodesia and Nyasaland are joined in the Central African Federation, but the federal legislature concerns itself only with matters of common interest to the three countries, leaving purely territorial affairs to the individual legislatures, and special provision is made in the federal constitution to safeguard African interests. There is no question that federation will greatly strengthen the economic stability and future development of all three countries, and thus benefit all their inhabitants, not least the African majority; but whilst this is recognized, Africans have yet to be reconciled to the possible political implications of the scheme as affecting themselves. In 1954 the first federal Cabinet had taken office under the federal Prime Minister, Sir Godfrey Huggins, formerly premier of Southern Rhodesia, and time, patience and statesmanship will be needed to justify this further stage in constitutional evolution, and especially to educate African opinion concerning it. It would certainly have had a better reception had this educational process been undertaken earlier.

The vast tract of country to which the name of Rhodesia was originally given in honour of its founder, Cecil Rhodes, was progressively brought under British influence in pursuance of his vision of a continuous extension of British territory stretching northwards from the Cape. Before the international scramble for African territory had fairly begun, Rhodes foresaw the possibilities of expansion to the north, and to carry out his great project, he formed the British South Africa Company, later known as the Chartered Company, in 1889. This is no place for an estimation of the remarkable if complex personality of Rhodes, which must be sought in his life and the history of the period, but there is no question of the greatness of his stature and the powerful impress which both his dreams and his actions have left upon the vast country which lies before his grave in the Matoppo hills.

That country also owes much to the work of a very different great man, David Livingstone, who explored all this region and beyond, discovering on the Zambesi the "smoke that thunders" which he named the Victoria Falls. Here stands his statue near the town of Livingstone which was named after him, and which was originally the capital of Northern Rhodesia until this was transferred to the more central position of Lusaka. The great ruins at Zimbabwe and other archaelogical remains suggest that an earlier civilization was once dominant here, but in the days of the Chartered Company the country had long been overrun by the Matabele, offshoots of the great Zulu race.

After long and complicated negotiations with King Lobengula, Rhodes set to work to forestall or buy up all other claims and to consolidate British interests through the Chartered Company. The next two or three years were occupied with the settlement of the country, but the first of the Matabele wars soon blazed up, and Lobengula was defeated at Buluwayo, the site of the present city. Later, Lobengula died, and Matabeleland was eventually reduced to order, though a further uprising took place in 1896, after the unfortunate Jameson raid in the Transvaal, but this was settled by the personal courage of Rhodes, who went unarmed to meet the Matabele impis in the Matoppos and gained their submission.

Progress was meanwhile made with the development of the country, with cultivation and mineral exploitation, railway and road construction and the settlement of towns, though all this was held up by the South African and later by the First World War. In 1911 the vast tract of country under the Company rule was divided into Southern and Northern Rhodesia, the latter being considerably the larger but much less suited for white settlement. After the First World War, the southern settlers began a movement for responsible government. The rights of the Chartered Company were bought out by the Crown in 1918, and two years later, although offered the alternative of entering the Union of South Africa, the settlers voted for separate self-government for Southern Rhodesia.

Since 1923 Southern Rhodesia has carried on its own government with a Prime Minister and Cabinet and a parliament predominantly representative of the white settlers. It did not acquire "dominion" status, although its Prime Minister has attended Commonwealth Conferences and its affairs have been dealt with through the Commonwealth Relations and not the Colonial Office, because the British Government retains control of its external affairs and in theory, though not greatly in practice, of its native policy. In this, Southern Rhodesia is more liberal in its attitude than South Africa, and may be said to stand roughly half-way between the "apartheid" policy of the Union and the colonial policy of the British Government; but looking to the future, if the Central African Federation, in which Southern Rhodesia is the principal partner, is to succeed, it must incline more definitely towards the British point of view. It is true that the three territorial governments continue to control separately their own affairs, and African interests are specifically safeguarded under the federal constitution, but the practice and example of Southern Rhodesia is bound to exercise a powerful influence outside its borders (as unfortunately South African policy does throughout the continent, including Rhodesia) and considerable qualities of tolerance and cooperation are called for from its European population, and of statesmanship from its government.

The European population of Southern Rhodesia numbers some 80,000 and the Africans 1,500,000. The franchise is in practice largely confined to the white settlers, though by the terms of the constitution Africans can acquire the franchise on the same terms as Europeans. Until recently the required qualifications have made this difficult, but nowadays more Africans are qualifying, the conditions have been eased, and if enfranchisement is made progressively possible for growing numbers of Africans, a solution may be in sight. The capital of Southern Rhodesia is Salisbury, which is also the federal centre, and Buluwayo (where the Rhodes Exhibition was held in 1953) and Umtali are other large towns. The Zambesi is its northern boundary.

Northern Rhodesia is however nearly double the size of its southern neighbour, stretching from the Zambesi to the Congo and covering nearly 290,000 square miles. It is primarily an African country, the white population numbering only some 20,000 mainly in the area of the copper mines, and the Africans nearly 2,000,000. It still has a Crown colony form of government, though the elected members are in a majority and several Europeans hold executive portfolios for groups of departments. Although the territory holds considerable possibilities for agricultural development and for the further cultivation of its chief crops, maize, tobacco, coffee and wheat, its principal wealth lies in mineral exploitation, especially in its copper mines, which are among the largest in the world, vanadium, zinc, cobalt and tin are also produced. The Roan Antelope, Nkana and other copper mines in the north are closely associated with similar fields in the Katanga and other areas of the adjoining Belgian Congo and this may lead to close co-operation between the two countries.

Northern Rhodesia is already the third largest copper producer in the world, but further mines have now been opened. This industrial development has however brought labour difficulties in its train, and while the companies have done much for both its European and African labour force, the white miners' unions have been jealous of African encroachment upon the skilled ranks. The Africans, who are also organized, are now however, being given more facilities for training, and it is in this direction, and in the extension by the Government of education and other measures of improvement among its African population, that future progress must lie. It is an encouraging sign that the new University College of Central Africa, towards the cost of which the British Government has made a substantial contribution, is inter-racial in scope.

The Barotseland province is a native reserve ruled over by a paramount chief assisted by a native council. The Bledisloe Commission, which had been primarily concerned with an earlier question of amalgamation, an issue which has now been determined by the federation of the three territories, also contemplated the eventual inclusion within Rhodesian territory of the northern portion of the Bechuanaland protectorate, a matter to which further reference will be made under the head of the High Commission territories.

NYASALAND

Adjoining the eastern boundary of Northern Rhodesia, the Nyasaland protectorate lies in a long narrow strip 38,000 square miles in area along the western border of Lake Nyasa. It is an equatorial region and except on the Shire highlands is unsuited for white settlement. The Bledisloe Commission had recommended in 1939 its amalgamation with Northern Rhodesia, but it preserves its separate government under the present federation.

The country had a turbulent history in the past, the small British settlement forming the African Lakes Trading Corporation having to contend constantly against Arab opposition, the slave trade and native uprisings. Order and peaceful development were however eventually brought to the territory. This fertile country has always been exceptionally populous and its surplus labour force has regularly migrated seasonally to other territories and as far afield as South Africa, though this movement is now regulated in the interests of the protectorate. Its principal exports, apart from labour, are tobacco and tea, but coffee, cotton and many other crops grow readily in its soil. Most of the trade of this whole Central African region including Nyasaland passes over the Zambesi bridge through the Portuguese East African port of Beira. The administrative centre of the protectorate Government is at Zomba, but the chief town is Blantyre. There are only some 3,000 Europeans, but the African population numbers nearly 2,500,000.

British Somaliland

From Central and East African territories, we now turn to the isolated British protectorate of Somaliland situated on the Horn of Africa facing across to Aden. It is bordered by Abyssinia and by French and Italian territory, and has an area of about 68,000 square miles. It was first occupied by Britain as the result of plundering raids on British shipping in 1827, and after various agreements with local sultans in subsequent years, it was finally declared a British protectorate in 1884. First administered as a dependency of India through Aden, it was transferred to the charge of the Foreign Office in 1898, and to that of the Colonial Office in 1905.

Somaliland has a turbulent history. The Somalis are of Arab stock and of nomadic habits, deriving their wealth mainly from cattle, sheep and goats, from the export of hides and skins, gum and resin and other products. The tribes are now peaceful and friendly, but there was formerly a strong fanatic element of dervishes who gathered under the banner of the Mad Mullah and for many years resisted successive expeditions sent against them up to and during the First World War, until finally their strength was broken with the flight of the Mullah into Abyssinia and his death there in 1921. Those tribes who had sought British protection were glad to be relieved of the persecution of the dervishes and the land settled down to peace and orderly progress, which was only interrupted by a temporary Italian occupation in 1940.

The climate is very hot especially on the coast, though more bracing on the inland plateau, but the country is arid and there is little rain. The capital is at Berbera on the coast, which has the only good harbour, and other towns are Zeilah and Hargeisa, the population of all fluctuating according to the season. Though motor roads and transport are making headway, the camel is still largely used. The defence of the country is mainly entrusted to the famous Somaliland Camel Corps, organized and led by British officers.

Most of the trade is with Aden. In early days administered by a Commissioner, the protectorate is now under a Governor with the usual type of Crown colony administration. The population is estimated at around 650,000.

THE HIGH COMMISSION TERRITORIES

or South African Protectorates, consist of Basutoland and Swaziland embedded within the territory of the Union and of the Bechuanaland protectorate on its northern border adjoining South West Africa. These countries are still British protectorates, and although under the South Africa Act of 1909 it was contemplated that they would eventually be handed over to the Union, conditions in South Africa at that time were very different to what they are today and in any case Britain is bound before any such transfer to consult the wishes of the inhabitants. Since the Statute of Westminster of 1931, followed by the South Africa Status Act of 1934, the Union has become completely independent of the United Kingdom, and its native policy to say the least has not recommended it to the peoples of the protectorates. We cannot therefore escape the moral responsibility assumed when we made treaties with their chiefs taking the countries under British protection at their own request, and this is in line with our general colonial policy of trusteeship.

The countries are therefore administered by a High Commissioner (who is also the British representative in South Africa) and he acts through a Resident Commissioner in each territory. In London, their affairs are dealt with through the

Commonwealth Relations office and not the Colonial Office, an arrangement which has not always proved beneficial to the territories, Both geographically and economically, however, they certainly form part of the Union system (except perhaps Northern Bechuanaland) and the Union Government is pressing for their early transfer. We are therefore confronted with a somewhat delicate problem. On the administrative level, South Africa is already co-operating to some extent with the responsible British officials, and the problem should not prove beyond solution if only time be granted and a sympathetic and statesmanlike approach is made on both sides.

Between them, the three countries cover a considerable area: Bechuanaland, by far the largest, extends over 275,000 square miles, Basutoland has an area of 11,716 square miles, and Swaziland 6,705 square miles. Including a considerable body of migrant labour among the Basutos who are always absent in the Union, the total population of the three countries is something over 1,000,000.

Bechuanaland in early days was associated with the missionary labours of Moffat and Livingstone and with the long rule of the great Bechuana chief Khama. Continual encroachments by the Dutch and attempts to establish Boer rule over the country brought repeated appeals from the people for British protection, and eventually in 1884 the wishes of the Bechuanas were granted. Bechuanaland is largely a pastoral country, its wealth being chiefly in cattle, the slight and even rainfall making agriculture an uncertain and hazardous undertaking. The climate is healthy, but the country suffers greatly from erosion, part of it being the great Kalahari desert. Deforestation in the past is probably the cause of the deterioration of a once fertile land, and measures are now being taken to combat and reverse this process. A mixed commission, including Tshekedi Khama, an outstanding personality in the Bamangwato tribe and himself a very successful stockraiser in the country, has recommended a development scheme which is now being proceeded with and of which irrigation is an essential part.

Local and tribal affairs are left largely in the hands of the various tribal chiefs assisted by their kgotlas or councils and acting in association with the British administrative officials. In the case of the Bamangwato tribe, however, there have been both internal dissensions and differences with the British authorities, the chief Seretse Khama, nephew of Tshekedi, having married an Englishwoman without previous consultation either with the tribe or with Government. Seretse is in exile and the succession to the chieftainship has yet to be determined. The headquarters of the administration are at Mafeking in Union territory, and this obviously has its drawbacks. The future of Bechuanaland is uncertain, but the northern portion at least might more appropriately be associated with the Central African Federation than with the Union.

Basutoland, "the Switzerland of South Africa", is situated in the Drakensburg range and is entirely surrounded by Union territory, in which it forms a native island, for neither here nor in the other protectorates are white settlers encouraged. It is a beautiful and picturesque country and the Basutos, like most mountaineers, are an independent and warlike race. Their great leader in the past, Moshesh, fought off the Zulus under Chaka and Moselikatze, and subsequently encouraged the work of the missionaries, when many of the people became Christians.

The Basutos also had trouble with the Boers, and eventually Moshesh appealed to Britain, saying "Let me and my people rest and live under the wide folds of the British flag before I am no more". The appeal was granted and the country became British territory in 1868, the Basutos being received as British subjects and not as protected persons. They still hold that status, although the present protectorate was declared in 1884 after an unsuccessful attempt to bring the land under the Cape Colony. The Basutos have never been an easy or tractable people to deal with, but they are satisfied with their present status, in which they enjoy a large measure of liberty and local self-government, and are extremely reluctant to relinquish it for Union control, even though their trade is entirely dependent upon the Union and a large number of their menfolk work in the Rand mines and other parts of South Africa.

The capital is at Maseru, which has rail connexion with the South African system. There is a Native Council of 100 members with the paramount chief acting as chairman. The country is very fertile and produces good grain crops. Cattle, sheep and goats, mohair and wool, wheat and hides are among the exports. The Basuto pony, which is also bred, is famous for its strength and endurance.

Swaziland, the smallest of the three territories, lies between Natal, the Transvaal and Portuguese East Africa. The Boers forced the country to make many concessions, and the Swazis, siding with the British in the South African war, were at their request brought under British protection. The capital is at Mbabane, and the people enjoy a large measure of tribal autonomy, though here there are several thousand white settlers to about 200,000 Africans. Like the Basutos, many of the Swazis also work in the South African mines. Swaziland is largely pastoral, but maize, tobacco and cotton are also grown, and there are valuable mineral deposits, especially tin. The country is well served with motor roads and transport. The Resident Commissioner has an advisory council representing the settlers and a Native Council composed of the indunas of the nation under the paramount chief.

In all three territories a series of economic investigations were carried out, as the result of which various development schemes have been undertaken. The chief need of Bechuanaland has always been an assured water-supply and countererosion measures, and the latter also applies in Basutoland. Improved methods of cultivation and cattle-breeding, irrigation, marketing, medical and educational services have also been carried out with the aid of Development and Welfare funds, but many of the people are intensely conservative in their ways and their co-operation is essential.

The British colonies in Africa, which we have now briefly surveyed, form part of the problem of Africa as a whole. As we have already seen, for both physical and political reasons, Africa has been late in its emergence into modern civilization and it has still considerable leeway to make up. But both world wars made a powerful impact upon the African peoples who took an active part in the campaigns both within and beyond Africa. For most of them it was their first glimpse of the world beyond their native villages and besides meeting fellow Africans and other peoples, they were trained in varied technical skills for which there was little demand on their return, nor could they settle down again to village life.

All Africa has long been continuously subjected to the intensive influence of European conditions and ideas, and in British territories particularly our policy of education and training for self-government, and our own example and institutions, have had considerable effect, especially upon educated Africans, whose talents have not been sufficiently enlisted in the service of their countries. The upsurge of nationalism amongst politically backward peoples everywhere has had its full effect in Africa, and while the example of the more politically advanced communities in West Africa has naturally impressed Africans throughout the continent, they have also noted the opposite trend of the *apartheid* movement in South Africa. The Union is an independent nation of the Commonwealth and other Commonwealth countries cannot perhaps fully appreciate or understand South African problems, which in any case are beyond the scope of this book, but we in Britain, because of our extensive responsibilities in Africa, cannot escape serious concern with what takes place in South Africa in view of its inevitable repercussions throughout British colonial Africa.

Africa is a whole and its problems, physical, economic, social and political, cut across all artificial boundaries. The locust and the tsetse-fly and other pests and diseases do not respect political divisions, nor certainly in this modern age can the flow of ideas be restricted. In the scientific, technical and administrative spheres, co-operation is fortunately making great progress. All the colonial powers and South Africa have concerted schemes for international co-operation, and not only the locust and the tsetse-fly are thus subjected to combined attack, but in agriculture, health, medicine, methods of administration and many other departments, there is constant and growing consultation and co-ordination.

Beyond all this, however, the human and political problem remains. In the plural or multiracial communities, that problem can only be solved on the basis of partnership and friendly co-operation between the races, the methods and implications of which must be worked out by all the inhabitants of each territory. Africa cannot be reserved only for the African peoples and it would be very bad for them if it could. Europeans are in Africa to stay and they have a very important role to play there if they can find an acceptable means of doing this in conjunction with the African peoples themselves. No one race, either white or black, can be dominant over others in Africa. Rhodes long ago declared the basic principle of "equal rights for every civilized man" and Milner had also said "Not race nor colour but civilization is the test of political rights".

Obviously everything depends upon the interpretation of "civilization" in this context, but Britain at least is set upon the right path in its policy of education and training for self-government. Can this be implemented in time, or will the impatience of Africans endanger the future? We have a heavy responsibility to try and control the pace in the best interests of the mass of the African peoples, but African leaders have at least an equal responsibility.

Africa however is largely a political jig-saw puzzle and other colonial powers in Africa have not the same policy or methods as Britain, to say nothing of indigenous African states. If dangers and tensions are to be avoided in the future, some consultation must take place in the political as in the technical and administrative spheres, from which indeed it might develop naturally. In that connexion the future of West Africans as a whole, both British and French, presents a problem for consideration. Lord Hailey in his *African Survey* and many subsequent reports and investigations have indicated the many directions in which co-operation would be fruitful, but it may be necessary to envisage a future international Council of Africa, upon which not only colonial and other powers but African countries already independent or moving towards self-government would be fully represented. Such a Council, whilst not relieving the present authorities of their responsibilities until their mission can be completed, but at the same time urging full co-operation between them, should look to a future when the natural aspirations of African peoples of all races can be eventually satisfied. This is indeed a world problem.

CHAPTER V

MEDITERRANEAN AND INDIAN OCEANS

GREAT BRITAIN in the days of the Empire established herself in the Mediterranean primarily for strategic reasons. It was part of her great highway to India and Australasia, the lifeline of Empire, and to the Commonwealth even in these changed days, it remains an essential line of communication. Before the Suez canal was cut, all shipping had to go round the Cape, which therefore became a British base in earlier days, and in the Second World War it was demonstrated that the Cape route could be used again, but naturally the Suez canal and Red Sea route is easier and shorter, and consequently Britain has her outposts at Gibraltar, commanding the western entrance, at Malta in a central position near Sicily, and at Cyprus in the eastern Mediterranean about 250 miles north of the mouth of the canal and close to the Turkish mainland.

For similar reasons Britain has necessarily maintained close relations with Egypt, which must ultimately become owner of the canal, and has meanwhile kept a force at the Canal base to protect communications in time of war. The future of the present base is a matter between Britain and Egypt, but obviously the maintenance of such a vital means of communication in any emergency is a serious responsibility which must be met unless it can be adequately controlled from Cyprus or south of the Red Sea. Aden with its extensive protectorate along the south coast of Arabia falls within the same sphere of influence and leads on to the Indian Ocean. (We have now agreed with Egypt.)

GIBRALTAR

The great fortress rock of Gibraltar stands sentinel over the western entrance to the Mediterranean, an impressive symbol of the once mighty British naval power which guarded the seaways of the world. In ancient days it was one of the Pillars of

Hercules, known as Mons Calpe, and its present name is derived from the Arabic Jebel Tarik. The Rock is some two and a half miles in length and about three-quarters in breadth, and rises gradually to a height of 1,400 feet, the steepest side facing the Mediterranean. The town and harbour face across the bay and by means of extensive moles a large water space, sufficient to meet all the needs of the Fleet and mercantile shipping, has been enclosed. The Rock is strongly fortified.

Until the fifteenth century it remained under the dominion of the Moors, after which it became part of the kingdom of Granada. During the war of the Spanish Succession, it was captured by a British force under Admiral Sir George Rooke in 1704 and its possession was confirmed to Britain by the Treaty of Utrecht in 1713. Several unsuccessful attempts were made to recapture it, and in 1779 it was subjected to a great siege which lasted four years, but all assaults were heroically withstood by the garrison under Lord Heathfield with the help of the Fleet, which finally, under Lord Howe, won a great victory at sea and raised the siege in 1783.

The British title to Gibraltar, however, rests upon a better basis than capture in war, quite apart from two and a half centuries of occupation; for by the Treaty of Versailles of 1783, renewing the Treaty of Utrecht, Spain relinquished for ever all rights in Gibraltar, in return for which she received extremely handsome compensation, for we handed over not only Minorca, still in Spanish possession, but also Florida, which she subsequently sold advantageously to the United States.

There is therefore not the slightest foundation in history for any Spanish claim that may be put forward, usually for propaganda purposes, to Gibraltar. Geographically it may doubtless be said to form part of the Iberian peninsula, but it is divided from the mainland by a sandy isthmus which is treated as neutral territory, and in any case the Iberian peninsula does not belong to Spain. Certainly the Portuguese have no slightest objection to Britain's possession of Gibraltar, nor for that matter have the Basques and Catalans or probably the great majority of the Spaniards. Indeed any change in its status would be unwelcome to the inhabitants of La Linea and the adjacent territory many of whom work in Gibraltar and who derive much benefit from the British occupation. The necessarily restricted civil population of Gibraltar, about 23,000 in number, are not themselves Spanish.

Being primarily a fortress and naval station rather than a colony, the Governor of Gibraltar is also the General commanding the garrison. He is aided by an executive council, but the affairs of the town are in the hands of a popularly elected City Council. The climate is healthy and Gibraltar is a popular tourist resort and a busy trading centre, being virtually a free port. The revenue is derived from import duties, Crown rents, licence fees and port dues.

Education is compulsory, and public health and civic affairs are well looked after. The town is modern and has some fine buildings and other amenities. The water supply is largely dependent upon the rains and is stored in underground tanks hewn out of the solid rock.

Whether in fact Gibraltar would be able properly to fulfil its function in any future war, it is very difficult to say, but the same doubt applies in some measure to other similar fortresses.

Malta

The George Cross island in the central Mediterranean 80 miles south of Sicily and about 200 miles north of Tripoli, is an important naval station and dockyard and headquarters of the now somewhat diminished Mediterranean Fleet but it is also a self-governing colony.

It has been claimed for the Maltese that they are the smallest nation with the longest history in the world. Certainly the little Maltese group, comprising Malta, Gozo and Comino, together the size of the Isle of Wight, can show a continuous history from the Stone Age down to the present day, and like the sister island of Cyprus in the Eastern Mediterranean, it epitomizes in its own story the whole history of the Middle sea in western civilization. Phoenicians, Carthaginians, Romans, Arabs, Normans, Sicilians, Castilians, the famous Knights of Malta, the French and finally the British have all left their mark in turn on the islands, but the Maltese people have preserved their racial integrity through every change, with their own language and culture, a language unique in Europe and akin in many respects to Arabic.

Under the Phoenicians, Malta became an important colony and one of the principal depots of Phoenician trade. To them succeeded the Carthaginians who held the island until the second Punic war, when it passed to Rome. The Roman rule endured for nearly a thousand years and much of it was a period of great prosperity for the island, when magnificent temples, mansions, baths and other evidences of Roman civilization were built, though unfortunately few relics of this period remain. The island, then known as Melita, was the scene of the shipwreck in 58 A.D. of St. Paul, who converted the people to Christianity, which they retained through all subsequent vicissitudes. The smaller island of Gozo is known in Greek legend as Calypso's isle, from the story of Telemachus in the Odyssey.

After a period of disorder following the fall of the Roman Empire, the Saracens became lords of the island in 870 and it remained under Arab rule until 1090 when the Norman Count Roger of Sicily defeated the Saracens and Malta became part of the Sicilian kingdom. After his death a turbulent period of some centuries ensued, when Angevins, Aragonese and Castilians ruled Sicily and Malta in succession, but this period was brought to an end about 1550, when the Emperor Charles V, at the Pope's instigation, granted Malta and Gozo to the Knights of the Order of St. John of Jerusalem, who had been driven out of Rhodes by the Turks.

Then followed the golden age of Malta when, after becoming famous throughout Christendom for the heroic resistance of the Knights under their Grand Master, La Vallette, after whom Valletta is named, to the great siege of the Turks in 1565, the island drew wealth and support as a bulwark against Islam from all the countries of Europe, and was beautified and enriched with magnificent churches, palaces and fortifications, including the "auberges" of the nations still in use as public buildings in Valletta.

The Order however gradually decayed until in 1798 it collapsed before Napoleon. But the Maltese rebelled against the French and called in the assistance of the British, who defeated the French in 1800; and although Britain handed back the island to the Knights under the Treaty of Amiens, the Maltese insisted on the British staying, and to their joy and relief it was finally ceded to Britain under the Treaty of Paris, 1814. The Maltese have never been strong enough to preserve their independence, but although under successive conquerors they have played an active part in their local affairs, only under Britain, whose aid and protection they invited, have they attained self-government. Constitutional government on the British parliamentary model was first introduced in 1921, but owing to internal dissensions (chiefly due to Italian propaganda and religious difficulties) it had to be suspended in 1936. Later however it was restored, and the Maltese, on the basis of adult suffrage, became fully responsible for their own affairs, defence and foreign policy being naturally reserved to Britain. For economic reasons, the Maltese have since demanded closer association with Britain, and it is proposed to transfer responsibility for Malta from the Colonial Office to the Home Office, thus placing them on a somewhat similar footing to the Channel islands and the Isle of Man. For its heroic defence in the Second World War, Malta was awarded the George Cross, an honour of which it is justly proud.

The islands have a civil population of some 320,000, but this is more than their small natural resources can support. Much of Malta is barren and the soil, though closely cultivated, is thin and scarce. Gozo is more fertile. Oranges, potatoes, and other crops are grown, and the Maltese are skilled mechanics and craftsmen, hard and thrifty workmen and good fishermen. Maltese lace is deservedly famous and amongst other industries are button and pipe-making and brewing. The principal source of employment is, of course, the dockyard and naval establishments generally, but this is necessarily less than it has been in the past, and the population, being Roman Catholic, tends to outrun subsistence.

With the improvement of power supplies and other services, further industries are being encouraged. Britain voted large sums to Malta to repair the extensive destruction wrought in the island during the war, and this gave much additional employment for a time but is naturally coming to an end. Until the birth-rate can be modified, the only answer to the pressure of population, apart from the development of further industries including the tourist industry, is regular emigration. Fortunately the Maltese have always freely emigrated, especially to other countries of the Commonwealth and this movement is continuing, but the estimated present need is at least 8,000 per annum. Education is free and compulsory and Malta has its own University, founded in 1769 and well known in Europe. The Catholic Church is naturally a powerful institution in the island.

There is ample scope for the development of tourism in Malta. The climate is excellent in winter and not too hot in summer, living is comparatively cheap and there are many good hotels. Besides its picturesque towns, villages and churches, its scenic beauty, the magnificent Grand Harbour at Valletta, the palaces of the Knights, the auberges of the nations, the national museum and opera house and other attractions, Malta also possesses many interesting relics of the Stone Age, notably the famous Hypogeum at Hal Saflieni and the temples at Tarxien, which are amongst the archaeological wonders of the world. In Gozo also there are Stone Age temples at Gigantija. With the growth and cheapening of air and sea travel, and Malta's close ties with Britain, this delightful mid-Mediterranean island should become an increased objective for visitors from Britain and other parts of the Commonwealth.

This also is abundantly true of

CYPRUS

Known in classical legend as the birthplace of Aphrodite, Cyprus is a very beautiful island with an equable climate and, like Malta, possesses many monuments of historic beauty and archaeological interest. It is a land of varied and picturesque scenery with mountains rising to the 6,400-foot peak of Mount Troodos. The island has an area of about 3,600 square miles, being nearly 150 long by some 30 to 60 miles in breadth. In ancient times it was well wooded and supported a reputed population of a million, whereas now it has less than half that number, but this is considerably higher than when Britain took it over from Turkey in 1878. Its mineral wealth was well known to the Greeks and Romans, the name Cyprus deriving from the Greek word for copper. She still possesses copper, iron, chromium, asbestos, marble and probably other minerals. Cyprus is a wine-growing country and also produces oranges, olives and other fruits, tobacco, cotton, flax and vegetables.

The history of Cyprus, like that of Malta, presents a microcosm of Mediterranean civilization. England's first connexion with it was in the twelfth century, when Richard Lionheart conquered it and at Limassol married Berengaria of Navarre, but subsequently passed it on to the Knights Templars. Later for many generations the island lay desolate and almost depopulated under Turkish misrule, until 1878 when Disraeli at the Berlin Conference secured Turkish agreement to its occupation and administration by Britain, but as it still remained nominally a Turkish possession, tribute continued to be paid annually from local resources (though this probably should have been remitted by Britain) until Turkey entered the First World War against Britain when all tribute ceased and Cyprus became in 1925 a British colony.

The original object of the British occupation was to protect the Suez canal, but this was later achieved directly through Egypt itself and Cyprus suffered a further period of relative neglect, though many things were done to improve its parlous condition under Turkey. Now again Cyprus has come into prominence as an important strategic centre for the Eastern Mediterranean. It offers great possibilities as a naval and especially as an air base, for which the great central plain of Messaoria is very suitable.

Amongst many mediaeval monuments, there are fine Gothic churches in Nicosia and Famagusta, the Abbey of Bella Paise, the castle of St. Hilarion and many other remains. The climate is dry and healthy and the scenery especially in the mountain range is magnificent. The villages are picturesque, the people are kindly and hospitable and living is fairly cheap. Kyrenia in the mountains, in which many British people live, is cool in the hottest months. With improved access facilities, it is ideal in many respects both as a resort and for permanent residence, for which it offers many advantages.

The population of Cyprus is mainly of Greek extraction, though there is a fairly large Turkish Moslem minority. The great majority of the peasants, both Greek and Turkish, are mainly concerned with getting their living, which in the past was rendered more difficult by their backwardness and indebtedness to moneylenders, a double handicap which Britain has done a great deal to remove. But the more educated classes are, like Greeks everywhere, very politically minded, and a movement has grown up among them, strongly fostered for its own reasons by the Orthodox hierarchy in Cyprus, for Enosis or union with Greece. This is a very natural development in the cultural field, but some at least of its political colour (which springs from mixed causes) is due to lack of imaginative sympathy on the part of Britain. Greece herself views the movement with understandable reluctance, and if the island were indeed to be united to Greece, the result would probably prove beneficial to neither, nor even perhaps to some of its professed advocates. The Turkish Cypriots are naturally strongly opposed to the movement.

There is no reason why Cyprus should not attain, like Malta, a full measure of local self-government, when her highly intelligent people would find far fuller scope in the Commonwealth than as an impoverished province of Greece, with whom however the Greek Cypriots would be free to develop fuller cultural relations. A liberal constitution was indeed conferred upon them after their liberation from Turkey, but owing to political agitation in 1931, when Government House was burned down, this was suspended, but a measure of self-government has since been offered and that offer is still available. A suggestion has been put forward that, by arrangement with Greece, the Greek Cypriots might enjoy a double franchise, as British citizens in Cyprus and Greek citizens in Greece, but it is highly probable that with more imaginative handling in the past, their friendly co-operation could have been secured to Britain, and with progressive steps towards representative government within the Commonwealth, the cultural and "patriotic" aims of the Greek majority could also have been adequately realized. With mutual tolerance and understanding, it is still not too late to achieve this.

It is a pity that we have not sponsored in Cyprus, as in other colonies, a university such as even the small island of Malta possesses, and which might have drawn off some of the fervour devoted to politics and attracted the intellectuals who now go to Athens, Paris and other centres.

Cyprus however is benefiting greatly by development and welfare schemes, by land improvements, savings bank and co-operative schemes, irrigation, well-boring and tree-planting, by the elimination of malaria, by road construction, air developments and many other improvements; and it is permissible to hope that, as long as this lovely island is important to the Commonwealth, its future will be deservedly brighter than its past.

In earlier years, in dealing with British colonial affairs in the Mediterranean area, it would have been necessary here to refer to Palestine and Transjordan, and even to Iraq and Syria, but that chapter is closed, and independent states have arisen despite some troublous periods (especially in Palestine) and their history must be sought elsewhere. From Cyprus we now traverse the Suez canal and the Red Sea and arrive at Aden.

Aden

With its protectorate stretching across the south coast of Arabia, Aden guards the entrance to the Red Sea and the canal as Gibraltar forms the western gateway to the Mediterranean. Although it has been a British possession since 1839, it did not acquire Crown colony status until 1937, having previously been administered as a dependency of India.

Aden itself stands in a commanding position on the southwest point of Arabia at the head of the gulf, and looking across to the horn of Africa and British Somaliland, with which it trades. The peninsula forms a natural stronghold with rocks rising to nearly 1,800 feet and two harbours, the more important, on the western side, being known as Aden Back Bay. Of importance in ancient times as the sea terminus of the caravan routes across Arabia, and a junction of east and west, Aden declined after the development of the Cape route, but recovered its prestige after the opening of the Suez canal. It was ceded to Britain by a local sultan in 1899, when it appeared of little importance. It is now a busy coal and oil fuelling station and naval base. Most ships on the Red Sea route call at Aden and its free port is a busy distributing centre for the merchandise of Europe, Asia and Africa.

The colony includes the islands of Perim and Karaman in the Red Sea, and has an area of about 80 square miles with a population of about 100,000; but the protectorate extending from the kingdom of the Yemen along the southern Arabian coast to the sultanates of Muscat and Oman and including the island of Sokotra has a total area of 112,000 square miles and a population of around 700,000. It comprises a number of small sultanates in treaty relation with Britain and in the western portion the Hadhramaut, a region made familiar by the writings of Freya Stark and other travellers. British protection also extends over the Bahrain islands and the Kuria Muria group in the Persian Gulf. In fact, British prestige and influence in all this coastal region has a steadying effect upon somewhat unstable local populations and conditions.

The Aden peninsula is sun-scorched but not unhealthy. Its chief difficulty is a scanty rainfall, but the water supply has been greatly improved by storage and other measures. The colony has the usual form of Crown colony government and the town is under municipal administration. The greatest recent development has been the building of a large new oil refinery costing £50,000,000 for the Anglo-Iranian company.

We now enter the Indian ocean in which are several British island groups.

Mauritius

Lying about 500 miles east of Madagascar, Mauritius is a beautiful island, verdure clad, well-watered and mountainous in the interior, being volcanic in origin. It has an area of 720 square miles, measuring about 39 miles from north to south and 129 miles from east to west. The climate is very moist and tropical, especially at sea-level, and the European residents live mostly in the hills. Its principal industry is sugar, for the cultivation of which it is exceptionally well suited, and most of its more accessible surface is covered with sugar plantations; but realizing the danger of depending upon only one crop, the Mauritians have taken up secondary industries such as aloes, rum, copra, coconut oil, tea and tobacco.

The population of around 500,000 is composed of people of European, mainly French descent, termed creoles, and mixed Indian and African peoples brought there to cultivate the sugar plantations. The capital is Port Louis, with an excellent harbour and considerable trade, but the Europeans live chiefly in Curepipe, at an altitude of 1,800 feet, connected with the capital by rail.

Mauritius has an eventful history. Originally discovered by those indefatigable navigators the Portuguese in 1505, it was later colonized by the Dutch, who named it after their Stadtholder, Count Maurice. In 1710 however the Dutch abandoned the island, which was soon after taken over by the French East India Company and renamed Ile de France. About the same time the French colonized the neighbouring island of Reunion, then called Bourbon. In 1735 the Ile de France received its most famous Governor, Mahé de la Bourdonnais, whose fame is still perpetuated both in Mauritius and in the Seychelles. To his foresight and energy the island owed its later development and prosperity. He founded Port Louis, built roads and forts, cleared forests, and above all introduced sugar planting. He settled the country generally and was also responsible for much progress in the Seychelles, but enemies at home had him recalled and he died eventually a prisoner in the Bastille. His statue is in La Bourdonnais Square, Port Louis.

In 1767 the island passed from the company to the French Crown, and later during the Napoleonic wars was used as a base from which to attack British merchantmen. Accordingly the British fitted out an expedition in India which captured the island in 1810. By the Treaty of Paris 1814, it was formally ceded to Britain and its original name of Mauritius was restored. The French laws and customs, however, together with the language and the Catholic religion, were left undisturbed and

Mauritius remains largely French in character to this day, though in every way loyal to the British Crown. The administration is as elsewhere in process of transition by the addition of elected members, and the island has benefited by the expenditure of development and welfare funds on various schemes and public services.

There are various scattered island dependencies, including Rodriguez, with a population of over 12,000 and local industries, and the Chagos archipelago of which the principal island is Diego Garcia. The region is subject to hurricanes.

THE SEYCHELLES

These "pearls of the Indian Ocean", as they are deservedly and appropriately called, widely scattered as if loosened from the thread, lie about 970 miles east of Zanzibar. The centre and largest island of the group, which numbers over ninety islets, is Mahé, named after La Bourdonnais of Mauritius. The population is over 40,000 and the capital is Port Victoria on Mahé, with a good harbour, about 930 miles distant from Mauritius. The other islands include Praslin, La Digue, Silhouette, Felicité, Curieuse, North Island, Greticy, and many subsidiary groups.

The Seychelles were first settled from Mauritius and Reunion and have somewhat of the same French character, though the British element is here stronger. The original settlers were later reinforced by negroes, many of them freed from slavery by British warships, and by Indians and Chinese. Since it was used like Mauritius as a French base during the Napoleonic wars, it was also captured by the British and ceded in 1814. The Seychelles were also fortunate in a good French governor, de Quincy, originally appointed by King Louis XVI, who not only remained at his post throughout the Revolutionary and Napoleonic periods, but was actually confirmed in office by the British and eventually died in Mahé in 1827, having ruled over the islands to their great benefit for more than thirty-eight years.

The islands, which are very lovely and fertile, enjoy for the most part a healthy climate and offer many attractions to the visitor or for residence, since living is comparatively cheap. They have been likened to a maritime garden of Eden, and certainly few who visit them fail to succumb to their charm. Their principal industry consists in the products of the coconut, and Praslin grows the famous coco-de-mer or double coconut, which is unique. The fisheries form another staple industry, and guano is largely exported from some of the islands, together with cinnamon, vanilla and other products, including tortoise-shell. Giant turtles are common in the Aldabra group. Other potential resources are being exploited by various development schemes. The Governor is advised by small executive and legislative councils, both of which have unofficial members.

THE MALDIVE ISLANDS

lying far south of Ceylon, of which they were formerly a nominal dependency, form a very numerous group of small scattered islands of which Male is the administrative centre. Long ruled over by hereditary sultans who were magniloquently styled "lord of thirteen provinces and twelve thousand isles", the islanders, who are of Aryan or Sinhalese origin and Mohammedan by religion, are a hardy and seafaring race and keen traders, who have retained nearly all their original customs, traditions and laws, and virtual independence. They number about 100,000 and being accustomed to active participation in their own affairs, their sultans were obliged to be constitutional rulers, assisted by a people's Assembly and responsible ministers. Recently they formed themselves into a republic with their last sultan as first president but this experiment did not last long and they have now returned to the sultanate form of government to which they have been so long accustomed. The Maldives are now a British protectorate.

The history and picturesque customs of this isolated and independent community have been most readably described at first hand by Mr. T. W. Hockley in his book *The Two Thousand Isles*. The people are practised seafarers and voyage afar in their native sailing craft or buggalows. Male is some 400 miles from Colombo. The islands export coconut oil, coir, tortoiseshell and other products.

Scattered eastward across the Indian ocean are other islands such as the Cocos or Keeling group and Christmas island which are attached to Singapore, and with them we approach Malaya and the East, described in the following chapter.

CHAPTER VI

MALAYA AND THE EAST

In our voyage across the world from the West Indies to Malaya, we have definitely reached an Asian and eastern standpoint, and it is as well to remind ourselves of the political background to the British colonies in this region. It must be remembered that in point of numbers the Commonwealth as a whole is predominantly a community of coloured peoples, and it is in this eastern hemisphere that its most populous units are found. The three senior partners here are India, Pakistan and Ceylon, accounting between them for some 450,000,000 people still steadily increasing. Burma too was formerly within the British sphere, but elected for independence outside the Commonwealth, though she could have secured all she needed within it, together with economic and other advantages. It is possible that she may revert to closer association with the Commonwealth in the future.

Beyond these countries loom the vast masses of the new China, of 100,000,000 Japanese confined within their small islands, and of the great expanse of Soviet Russia stretching across Asia into Europe, to say nothing of the uneasy peoples of Indo-China. This is the region of the world where racial, political and ideological tensions are greatest and where many problems exist for the Commonwealth in the future. In China, communism is a force which may well be modified by the traditional characteristics of the Chinese people, while the Indian sub-continent forms for the Commonwealth a bridge between east and west.

Malaya

British Malaya forms a long peninsula stretching south-east from Siam to its tip at Singapore and divided from Indonesia by the Straits of Malacca. It comprises the Straits Settlements and the nine Malay states now united in the Federation of Malaya. The Straits Settlements consist of Singapore, Penang, Malacca and Labuan, with various islands. The Malay states are Perak, Selangor, Negri Sembilan, Pahang, Johore, Kedah, Kelantan, Trengganu and Perlis. Borneo will be referred to separately. The total area is some 55,000 square miles, and the population, comprising Malays, Chinese, Indians and Eurasians, with about 40,000 Europeans, numbers around 6,500,000, including Singapore. The two principal races, Malays and Chinese, are about equal in number.

Malaya will always be associated in English history with the great name of Stamford Raffles, whose prescience first saw the potential importance of Singapore, then an uninhabited island off the coast of Johore in the extreme south of the Peninsula. In 1819 he persuaded the local sultan to cede it to Britain. Europeans had however obtained a foothold in Malaya in the sixteenth century, first the Portuguese at Malacca, attracted by the spice trade, and later the Dutch in 1641. The British did not appear until 1768, when Penang was ceded by the Sultan of Kedah to the East India Company, and Malacca fell later to the British in war. In 1826 the three settlements were placed under the Government of India, being transferred to the Colonial Office in 1867. Later, Cocos and Christmas islands were added, and Labuan off the coast of Borneo.

In 1874 the state of Perak accepted British protection, and this example was followed by Selangor, Pahang and a cluster of small states known as Negri Sembilan or the nine states. These four units agreed to federate in 1896 for public services and matters of common interest, and a federal centre was set up at Kuala Lumpur in Selangor, which was also the seat of the Federal Council. Siam was persuaded to transfer her suzerainty over the northern Malay states of Kelantan, Trengganu, Kedah and Perlis to Britain in 1909, and Johore in the south voluntarily accepted British protection in 1914. Although these states did not at first join in the federation, they did increasingly participate in the common administration of the peninsula, so much so that at one period there was a danger of over-centralization, and special steps were taken to preserve and strengthen local autonomy and to encourage initiative and practical experience in local government by the individual states.

The Malayan peninsula, thrust out, from the mass of Siam, Indo-China and Burma, has a mountainous backbone and is well irrigated by rivers from which the various Malay states take their names. Much of the interior is still covered by impenetrable jungle, in which some primitive tribes still roam; but the country is mainly inhabited by the Malays, who are believed to have made their way into the peninsula from the archipelago. Mohammedan by religion, they are expert fishermen and boat-builders living chiefly on the coasts and along the rivers. In the past they were greatly addicted to piracy and internecine warfare, and indeed the country has been completely transformed and modern Malaya is virtually a British creation.

The British suppressed piracy and intertribal warfare and gradually brought law and order to the whole peninsula. They have given Malaya a splendid system of communications in the Federated Malay States railways, comprising considerably over 1,000 miles of line connecting Singapore and Bangkok in Siam and all the intervening states and centres, and have built several thousand miles of excellent roads.

The wealth of Malaya today is entirely a modern creation. It is built up mainly on rubber and tin, and both these industries are recent developments, although Chinese had been working tin on a small scale for centuries. The Malays are a naturally courteous, hospitable and attractive people, but they are indolently inclined, and the introduction of new industries has brought with it a large influx of industrious Chinese, Indians and others, so that the Malays are at the moment actually outnumbered in their own country, which is faced with the problems of a plural community.

The story of the introduction of rubber into Malaya (and Ceylon) is a romance of science and commerce. The initiative was taken by Sir Joseph Hooker, then Director of the Royal Botanic Gardens at Kew. The hevea plant grew in a wild state in the forests of the Amazon and supplied sufficient rubber for the small needs of that day before the tremendous expansion in the uses of the material especially for modern transport. Henry Wickham, later knighted, was sent on collecting expeditions to Brazil, and it was due both to good fortune and to perseverance that some of the seeds were successfully transplanted and cultivated in Ceylon and Malaya. In Malaya the foundation of the industry was largely due to the patient pioneer efforts and ingenuity, despite initial apathy and discouragement, of Mr. Henry N. Ridley, then director of the Botanic Gardens at Singapore and Conservator of Forests for Malaya.

Malaya eventually became the largest producer of natural rubber in the world, and although it now has to meet competition from synthetic rubber, an industry built up during the war, rubber is still the mainstay of Malayan economy. So great was the production before the war that restriction schemes had to be introduced both for rubber and for tin, but even so, Malaya exported well over 360,000 tons annually. Malaya also produces about half the world's tin supplies, the mines being mainly worked and owned by Chinese. The tin resources of Malaya are very great and the country also produces other minerals such as coal, iron, manganese, lead and tungsten. The ancient staple industry consisted in the products of the coconut, and this is still important, but it is matched by the pineapple industry, Malaya being the second largest supplier in the world.

The oldest of the Straits Settlements is Penang, consisting of Penang island and Province Wellesley on the mainland commanding the western entrance to the Straits of Malacca. George Town is now a great free port like Singapore. Malacca was the first to attract Europeans, and the old town still holds many relics of Dutch and Portuguese days, though of late years its importance has relatively declined.

Singapore, however, is far and away the most important of the Settlements and for the present forms a separate administrative unit under its own Governor, although destined eventually to enter the Federation of Malaya. Since its foundation by Stamford Raffles, it has grown, as he foresaw, to be one of the greatest ports in the world. As a free port, it is the entrepôt for all the transit trade of the East, and its harbour is always filled with the world's shipping. With a population of over

1,000,000 made up of every race, Singapore has become one of the greatest cities of the East, with a progressive municipality and harbour board, and many fine public buildings, including Raffles College and the Medical College, together the nucleus of the University of Malaya.

The Singapore naval, military and air base was built out of the jungle and strongly fortified and equipped, though unfortunately it was unable to resist an unexpected landward invasion down the peninsula by the Japanese during the war. It possesses huge graving and floating docks, and facilities for repair, extensive military and civil establishments and one of the finest air-bases in the East. The Malay rulers and peoples, as well as Hong Kong, Australia and New Zealand, contributed substantially towards the cost of construction. The great civil airport adjoining is an important junction for British, American and Dutch air-lines, connecting with Britain, Holland, India, Indonesia, Kong Hong, Australia and New Zealand. Besides Singapore, Penang and Kuala Lumpur, other large centres include Ipoh in the tin-mining district, Taiping, Seremban, Johore Bahru and Port Swettenham.

Upon this thriving and prosperous country fell the disaster of the Second World War. Britain, with her defences and communications throughout the world stretched to the uttermost, was unable to prevent a Japanese incursion in force through Siam and down the length of the peninsula, and at the same time heavy local naval losses were incurred. The Japanese were therefore able to overrun the country and the Singapore base for a time, and although eventually defeated, left their mark in the resulting disorders which persisted after the war fomented by communist infiltration and organized banditry in the jungle. The long-protracted military emergency proved a great strain on the country, but eventually, under the energetic campaign directed by General Sir Richard Templer, it was got in hand, aided by the loyal co-operation of both Malays and Chinese, and civil order and rehabilitation is being steadily built up.

Despite the strain of the emergency, the declared policy of preparing the country for eventual self-government, though necessarily retarded for a time, was not lost sight of, and as the emergency was overcome, it was possible to make further progress in the political sphere. The difficulty in Malaya has been the welding together of the different racial communities, and the preserving of a fair balance between them. Britain has naturally felt a special responsibility for the Malay peoples, since it is their country, but the Chinese especially and the Indians have undoubtedly contributed greatly to the development of the country. Hitherto the Chinese have been regarded as immigrants without a permanent stake in the country, but now the considerable number of Straits-born Chinese and others are tending to settle down as Malayan citizens, which recent legislation enables them increasingly to do; and whilst formerly there was friction between the various racial communities, this is now giving way to a growing movement of co-operation between them towards a common aim of Malayan nationalism, which owes much to enlightened leadership on the part of both Malay and Chinese communities. There is now hope of the eventual building up, with Government encouragement, of a united Malayan nation.

Federation in Malaya may be said to have got off to a false start, for shortly after the end of the war, Sir Harold Macmichel was sent by the Colonial Office on a special mission to Malaya to propose Malayan Union, but although he succeeded at first in obtaining the assent of the Sultans, this gave rise to considerable popular criticism and to some disclaimers, and seeing their mistake the home authorities modified their proposals in favour of a Malayan Federation, taking in all the states but leaving them a measure of local autonomy. The federal legislation provided for Malayan citizenship for all races and their proportionate representation in the legislative council, for a Governor of the Federation with headquarters at Kuala Lumpur, and for the present a separate Governor of Singapore, both of whom come under the Commissioner-General for South-East Asia, whose jurisdiction also extends to Borneo. Singapore has also introduced a representative elected element into its legislative council. The whole of this region is in ferment, with the virtual independence of the Netherlands Indies, and the nascent but still uneasy nationalism of Indonesia; but there is no reason why Malaya should not eventually win through to a stable and assured future on a self-governing basis in the Commonwealth.

BORNEO

The great island of Borneo was largely colonized by the Dutch, but contains also three British territories in the north and north-east, namely British North Borneo, Brunei and Sarawak. The trade throughout the archipelago was long monopolized by the Dutch, and the British did not secure a permanent foothold in Borneo until the early nineteenth century. During the Napoleonic wars, however, Java and Sumatra themselves came for a time under British control and profited greatly by the enlightened and liberal administration of Sir Stamford Raffles, at that time governing Malaya, but they were subsequently handed back to the Dutch who, hostile then, to his reforms, long after acknowledged their indebtedness to Raffles.

Brunei, now the smallest of the three British territories in Borneo, and administered like Labuan with the Straits Settlements, was once a great Bornean State and held sway over what are now British North Borneo and Sarawak, and over Labuan and other tributaries. But its power decayed, hastened by piracy and internal strife, and it lost control of all its territories, save a mere 2,500 square miles, and in 1888 it gladly accepted British protection. Oil production is now being developed and already reaches over 5,000,000 tons annually.

Piracy and rebellion in Borneo led to a romantic episode in British colonial history, the exploits of James Brooke and the long rule of the White Rajahs of Sarawak. Brooke, a retired officer of the East India Company, had inherited a fortune and decided to travel, fitting out a yacht for that purpose and voyaging through the East Indian archipelago. In 1839 he offered his help to the Sultan in quelling a revolt in the Sarawak province and was so successful that he was appointed Rajah of Sarawak. He then set to work to introduce law and order into that country and to clear the seas of the ferocious pirates who made peaceful commerce impossible. This proved a formidable task in which he was allowed to receive the help of officers commanding British warships stationed in those waters, amongst whom was Captain, afterwards Admiral, Sir Harry Keppel. The campaign was fierce and protracted, but at last the pirates were destroyed in their lairs, and in 1844 the seas were clear.

Rajah Brooke still had trouble with the Chinese and some of the more turbulent tribes of the interior before he could settle down to peaceful rule. The province which he first took over was but 7,000 square miles in extent, but by successive concessions and purchases, Sarawak, whose complete independence was recognized in 1864, was enlarged to an area of some 50,000 square miles. The Brooke family were recognized as hereditary Rajahs by the British Government in 1904, a protectorate having been established over the whole of north Borneo, including Brunei and Sarawak, in 1888. For over a century the Brooke family ruled paternally over the country which their enterprising ancestor had pacified and settled, putting first the interests of the inhabitants and developing the country peacefully.

Latterly they had called in the assistance of a legislative council representative of the various elements of the people; but after the war, it was felt necessary for the full development of the country and in accordance with general colonial policy, in this region, to transform the country into a British colony, preserving the rights of the people to eventual self-government, and bringing it into line with the adjacent territory of British North Borneo. Thus came to an end a colourful chapter in British individual enterprise, the record of which, in the history of Sarawak and the Brooke family, will well repay further study: some sources are indicated in the bibliography.

Sarawak is a mountainous country, much of the interior being covered by dense forests penetrated by numerous rivers which form the natural highways. The total population is about 575,000, and the capital is Kuching, other important towns being Sibro and Miri, the latter the headquarters of the oilfields district. The country has made steady progress in commerce and peaceful development, and further economic schemes are being aided by development and welfare funds. Rubber is cultivated, and sago, and coal and other minerals are worked, but the most valuable product is petroleum, the administration levying a royalty on the steadily increasing output.

The remaining British territory in the island is British North Borneo, which until recent years was administered by a Chartered Company. The British North Borneo Company was formed in 1878 by amongst others Sir Alfred Dent and Admiral Sir Harry Keppel, and received its charter in 1881. The original concession was granted by the Sultan of Sulu, and this was later added to by concessions from the Sultan of Brunei. Subject to a Court of Directors in London, the country was ruled by a Governor whose appointment was approved by the Secretary of State for the Colonies, After the war, however, as in the case of Sarawak, the Company's Charter was terminated and compensation awarded, and the country was taken over as a British colony, with the usual colonial form of administration.

The territory comprises an area of some 30,000 square miles and the capital is at Sandakan. The population numbers some 340,000, mainly of Malay origin and Mohammedan in religion, The principal industries are rubber and timber, with copra, cutch and other products, and coal and iron ore are also worked. Besides Sandakan, the principal towns are Jesselton, the headquarters of the Government railway, Beaufort and Melalop. Both Sandakan and Jesselton have good harbours.

The British territories in Borneo suffered temporarily during the war, but the damage was repaired and orderly progress is now being made in social and economic development. Like Malaya, they come under the jurisdiction of the Commissioner-General for South-East Asia.

Hong Kong

From its commanding position in relation to the mainland, Hong Kong has been justly called "the gateway to China" and that indeed in the past has been its natural role. Whatever may be its political future, it has a vital part to play in the economy and communications of the vast country with which its trade and prosperity are indissolubly linked, and to which its existence and manifold activities under British administration have so far proved on the whole at least as beneficial as to Britain and the Commonwealth.

The importance of its spacious sheltered harbour was first seen during the war with China in 1839-42, but apart from its strategic position, the immense commercial possibilities of the place were soon realized, and the island of Hong Kong was ceded to Britain as one result of the war. But although thus born of conflict, it has indubitably since rendered great service to China and to the Chinese people, besides promoting Anglo-Chinese trade.

At the time of its cession, the island was practically uninhabited except for a few fishermen and was a barren and mountainous rock rising to a height of 1,800 feet in the centre. In itself at the time, it was certainly no loss to China, and what it has since become is entirely a British creation. Today the population of the colony, including the leased territory of Kowloon on the mainland, is nearly 3,000,000. The island has an area of only 32 square miles, but the Kowloon peninsula and the leased territory bring the total area up to about 390 square miles. The leased territory was acquired for a term of 99 years in 1898, and it must therefore revert to China in 1997, but as it would be very difficult for the island today to subsist separately without the mainland, the future of the colony must come up for settlement either then or earlier, and it is to be hoped that it can be settled by friendly agreement between the two countries.

Hong Kong is the name of the colony, but the town on the island is Victoria. Seen from the sea, especially at night, Victoria is a fine spectacle, since it rises from the magnificent harbour in tier after tier up the slopes of Victoria Peak, the shipping business and Chinese quarters encircling the harbour facing the mainland, then at a higher level the Government and other public buildings and parks and gardens, and finally the residential quarters climbing to the hill-tops. When all these terraces and buildings are illuminated at night, they make with the shipping in the harbour a galaxy of light rising to the stars. Much has been done by afforestation to clothe the barren rock and improve climatic conditions, and Victoria today, with its public services and amenities, is a handsome modern city, a great free port like Singapore, and a fine naval dockyard and shipbuilding and repair base. It is also becoming to an increasing extent a busy and varied manufacturing centre with not only modern equipment but a naturally industrious and skilful population.

Most of the trade is of course of a transit character, the annual tonnage entering and clearing the harbour being of the order of some 45,000,000 tons, but this is supplemented by the naval and commercial docks, and the building, engineering and repairing facilities, besides the growing manufactures. Hong Kong is an unrivalled centre of communications, being a great cable and wireless terminal, having steamship connexions all over the Pacific and the East, and rail, road and river connexions with the rest of China. It is also an international airways terminal.

The colony's contribution has not been only material in the promotion of trade and industry; it has also brought settled order and good government to a prosperous and industrious Chinese community which in the past flocked in increasing numbers from the uncertainties and perils of the mainland to the safety of British rule. It has an efficient educational system, crowned by the University of Hong Kong, which has done much not only for the people of the colony but also for students from the mainland. The University was established in 1912, when that great colonial statesman, Lord, then Sir Frederick, Lugard was Governor of Hong Kong. It has flourishing faculties in arts, engineering and medicine, and has received substantial aid not only from the Government but also from the Rockefeller Foundation and the Rhodes Trust.

The Governor is assisted in his functions by executive and legislative councils, with both official and unofficial members, in which increasing representation is being given to the Chinese community. The colony had to be temporarily surrendered to the Japanese during the war, but on their defeat, British administration was restored and had to cope with a further influx from China, and has now more than regained its former order and prosperity.

CHAPTER VII

THE PACIFIC ISLANDS

THE last stage of our journey from the Caribbean brings us to the widely scattered island groups of the Pacific. It may perhaps be desirable to repeat that the existence of so many island outposts in all parts of the world is no evidence of a spirit of "grab" or of an Autolycan tendency for picking up unconsidered trifles about the globe, but the inevitable result of our once world-wide and dominant sea-power, which needed convenient harbours, fuelling and watering stations, or to establish a line of communication with widely separated territories, and later cable and telegraph (and now air) terminals. Moreover, the unremitting activities and explorations of sea captains and navigators from Elizabethan down to modern times, together with charting duties for the Admiralty, naturally brought many islands and other lands under the British flag. Many more came under our jurisdiction or fell to us as prizes of war than we eventually retained. Not a few peoples or rulers, in the Pacific as elsewhere, besought our protection, and many responsibilities were reluctantly and belatedly undertaken. Indeed, had we been really an aggressive and consistently acquisitive power, as we have been commonly represented, we might have reason (despite appearances to the contrary) to be astonished at our own moderation!

THE FIJI GROUP

The Fiji islands are about 1,000 miles from Auckland and 1,700 from Sydney. The two principal islands are Viti Levu, on which is situated the capital, Suva, and Vanua Levu, and these islands between them account for over 6,000 square miles of the 7,000 occupied by the whole archipelago, which comprises over 200 islets. In the past the Fijians, of Melanesian stock, had a warlike and savage reputation and were constantly engaged in intertribal warfare and cannibalism, which caused the islands to be long shunned by Europeans, though Tasman, Captain Cook, Bligh of the *Bounty*, and many other navigators visited them. They were however well situated for trade and sea communications, and during the American Civil War, settlers from Australia and New Zealand planted cotton and even attempted to set up a local government, for the islands enjoy a temperate climate; but the experiment did not prove a success.

Meanwhile an outstanding native chief had emerged in the person of Thakombau, who applied for British protection for the islands. This was at first refused, but on being more than once repeated, two commissioners were eventually despatched to investigate. The chiefs led by Thakombau offered to cede sovereignty in the islands, and Sir Hercules Robinson, then Governor of New South Wales, went to the islands to negotiate the terms, with the result that a deed of cession was executed by Thakombau and other chiefs on 10 October, 1874, transferring sovereignty of the whole group to the British Crown.

Since that day, the story of Fiji has been one of constant and remarkable progress. The Fijians, as soon as the curse of internecine strife was removed, responded to the new conditions, sloughed off their old savage practices and were largely converted to Christianity. An intelligent and adaptable people, they proved amenable to educational influences and training, being already good cultivators, skilled craftsmen, and expert fishermen. Moreover, under British rule, they have always retained a large measure of self-government through their own chieftains, who assemble periodically in the great council of chiefs. Their representatives sit in the legislature, which besides officials comprises both elected and nominated unofficial members, representing Europeans, Fijians and the now large Indian immigrant community. This elective trend is continuing.

The capital, originally Levuka, was early removed to Suva, which is now a handsome town with a fine harbour and modern public buildings. The population both of Fiji and of the Western Pacific group exceeds 500,000, and while in Fiji the native Fijians still lead, the Indians are steadily increasing in numbers. They were originally imported to cultivate the sugar plantations, at which work they proved better than the native inhabitants. Cotton planting did not at first succeed, though it is now again being encouraged, but the introduction of sugar was so successful that it rapidly became, as it still is, the leading industry. This is followed by copra and other coconut products and by fruit, chiefly bananas; but the discovery and successful working of gold has led to its taking a very important place in the export trade.

Owing to its prosperity and peaceful development, Fiji is not only self-supporting but has built up a strong reserve fund, despite liberal expenditure on education, health and public works. Road construction in particular has been greatly developed and a fine circuminsular scenic road has been built round Viti Levu, the main island, which with other amenities and good hotels, has provided a strong and increasing tourist attraction to these beautiful islands.

The Fijian standard of living and culture has steadily risen. Fijians are excellent soldiers, as they have abundantly proved in war, and they are readily trained to skilled crafts and professions. The Central Medical School, which is famed throughout the South Seas and attracts recruits from other island groups, turns out native practitioners who do good work over a wide field in the Pacific. The island of Rotuma, 300 miles distant, has also formed part of the colony since 1880, being administered by a resident commissioner. It has a flourishing coconut industry.

Since Fiji was voluntarily ceded, Britain has a special trust for the Fijians, who are contented and loyal under British rule. With the development of air, sea and wireless communication, and the continued exploitation of its natural resources, Fiji bids fair to make even greater progress in the future than in the past. It will need to handle wisely its problem of a plural community, Fijian and Indian, but this is unlikely to present any great difficulty.

Formerly the Governor of Fiji was also High Commissioner for the Western Pacific, but after the war the headquarters of the Commission was removed from Suva to the Solomon Islands. The Governor of Fiji is, however, also responsible for Pitcairn and for the protectorate over the kingdom of Tonga.

The Gilbert and Ellice Group

The colony, which besides the Gilbert and Ellice group proper, includes Ocean, Christmas, Fanning and Washington islands, lies due north of Fiji. Originally a protectorate, the islands were formally constituted a colony at the request of the native chieftains in 1915. The Gilbert group consists of some sixteen islands and the Ellice group of nine small clusters. The total population is about 40,000, of whom only a few hundreds are Europeans, the native peoples being of Malayo-Polynesian race. The principal export is copra.

Each island has its own native council presided over by a native magistrate, and law and order are well maintained under the general supervision of the European administrative officials, who travel from island to island in their area. Much medical work has been undertaken, and a large central hospital is maintained at Tarawa in the Gilbert group, every island having its local hospital under the charge of a native student trained at Tarawa.

Ocean island, like Nauru shortly to be described, is rich in phosphates, and is worked by the British Phosphates Commission, which also works Nauru. Fanning island is the mid-Ocean station of the Pacific Cable Board. Christmas island is leased to the Central Pacific Coconut Plantations Ltd. Sea communications between all these groups of islands are maintained by the vessels of Burns, Philp & Co., those of the Phosphate Commission and others, and they are also connected by wireless telegraphy and telephony.

In the past the natives of these islands suffered greatly from the depredations of European "blackbirders", kidnappers of native labour, who took thousands of the inhabitants to work on plantations in Mexico and Guatemala, but with the coming of the British protectorate, these marauders were suppressed.

The British Solomons

The protectorate consists of a double chain of islands, extending from the Bougainville straits to the Santa Cruz group, a distance of over 900 miles, the total land area being around 11,000 square miles. The native population, mainly Melanesian, number about 100,000. The seat of government is at Tulagi, and the Resident Commissioner, representing the High Commission of the Western Pacific, which is also centred here, is assisted by a small Advisory Council, executive functions being exercised by District Officers, who travel constantly between the islands. Native headmen in the islands assist the administration.

These islands also suffered from the operations of "blackbirders", but the traffic was finally brought to an end. The Solomon islanders themselves, however, in the past carried on head-hunting and other inhuman practices, and were constantly engaged in savage inter-tribal feuds, until law and order were at length established. By 1900 a British protectorate had been extended over all the islands from Bougainville to Santa Cruz and from the Lord Howe group in the north to Rennell island in the south. The names of many of the islands, such as Guadalcanal, became prominent in the war against Japan, and the magnificent resistance put up by the islanders themselves against the Japanese demonstrated their loyalty to Britain. Apart from some material damage, which was soon repaired, the war did not leave them untouched, and much social and economic development is now being carried out in the islands.

The somewhat humid climate does not attract Europeans and comparatively few are resident in the islands, apart from officials. The principal products are coconuts, sandalwood, rubber, and various fruits.

Tonga

Captain Cook, who thrice visited these islands, received such kindness from the inhabitants that he called them the Friendly islands. They now form a native kingdom under British protection, the protectorate being established in 1900. There are three groups of islands, but the centre of government is on Tongatabu, the largest island in the group. The population of the group is around 40,000 and is still increasing.

The Tongans are Polynesians, intelligent, courteous and hospitable people, who take life easily. Formerly they carried on perpetual internecine warfare, but eventually an outstanding warrior and administrator emerged who established his authority over the whole group under the title of King Tubon I. In 1845 he opened the islands to various missionary bodies who converted the inhabitants to Christianity, and one of the missionaries became prime minister. King Tubon I died in 1893 and was succeeded by his grandson Tubon II, under whose rule the islands were placed by consent under British protection. On his death in 1918, Queen Salote succeeded. The Queen governs through a prime minister and a cabinet council composed of Tongans and Europeans, with a small legislative assembly. Queen Salote visited London in 1953 to attend the Coronation of Queen Elizabeth, and made appropriately a most friendly impression in the metropolis, and in return Queen Elizabeth visited Tonga on her voyage with the Duke of Edinburgh to New Zealand and Australia.

Life in Tonga is peaceful, the climate is healthy and there is no poverty or unemployment, since every Tongan is entitled to an allotment of land for his own cultivation, and the soil is fertile. Education is compulsory, and medical work and the public services are well organized. The people are good agriculturists and fishermen, and the chief exports are copra and bananas. On the whole, Tonga is a model South Sea island community, pursuing a tranquil and ordered existence under the protection of the British flag, and fortunately far removed, at least at present, from the strains and tensions which afflict the outer world.

THE PHOENIX GROUP

This consists of eight small islands, east of the Gilbert and Ellice group, which are not notable except that they happen to be well placed between Australia and America for air communication. The United States considered that they had some claim to certain of the islands, but by agreement between the British and American governments, an Anglo-American joint commission was set up in 1938 in respect of Canton and Enderbury islands, which are centrally situated and are suitable for air-bases which have been constructed on them. Some of the islands are leased to Burns, Philp & Co. for coconut cultivation.

PITCAIRN

Remote and isolated in the Pacific, Pitcairn is a rival to Tristan da Cunha in the Atlantic to be considered as "the loneliest isle", and it is also famous as the island chosen by the mutineers of the *Bounty* in 1789 as a refuge, after they had set Captain Bligh and a few companions adrift in the ship's boats. The whole dramatic story has been frequently told in print and filmed, and is the subject of a trilogy of novels by Nordhoff and Hall.

Under the leadership of Fletcher Christian, the mutineers first went to Tahiti, but fearing pursuit they eventually sailed, accompanied by Tahitian women, to Pitcairn, an island first discovered by a British ship in 1767. They reached Pitcairn in 1790 and remained undiscovered until an American ship found them in 1808, when most of the original mutineers were dead, but the little community had been brought through many privations by John Adams.

The community was later increased by men from other British ships, and after many tribulations, including removal for a time to Norfolk island, they settled down under their elected chief magistrate, who still bore the name of Christian. The island was brought under the jurisdiction of the High Commissioner for the Western Pacific in 1898, and now comes under the Governor of Fiji. Today the small community numbers some 200 souls and is self-supporting. The chief magistrate and a council of five are elected annually by all adults over eighteen years of age.

NAURU

Though but a small island some twelve miles in circumference, Nauru is valuable for its extensive phosphate deposits.

Originally annexed by Germany, it was surrendered to an Australian warship in the First World War, and is now a Commonwealth mandate, the administrator being at present appointed by Australia. The phosphate deposits, with those of Ocean island in the Gilbert and Ellice group, are worked by the British Phosphate Commission. These total over 500,000 tons annually and go chiefly to Australia and New Zealand.

The New Hebrides

Lying between the Solomon islands and Fiji, the New Hebrides are under joint administration by Britain and France according to the terms of the Convention of 1906. The arrangement in this instance has not been conspicuously successful, and the future régime of the islands deserves further consideration by the responsible powers.

First discovered by the Portuguese, the islands were given their present name by Captain Cook. Owing to disputes between British and French settlers and traders, a joint administration was decided upon as a way out of the difficulties. The total area of the group is about 5,700 square miles, but the climate is hot and damp and not very suitable for Europeans, though there are a small number of white people in the islands, mostly French: the native people, some 60,000 in all, are of Melanesian stock. Sandalwood, coffee, copra and other tropical products are exported, but the islands need further systematic development and a more settled form of administration.

In addition to all the territories great and small described in the foregoing chapters, for which Britain is primarily responsible, there are also some dependencies belonging to other members of the Commonwealth. Descriptions of these belong properly to works dealing with the responsible countries, and are beyond the scope of this volume, although some reference is made to them in the bibliography; but on the whole they are administered somewhat on the lines of British colonial policy, though without its specifically declared objective.

Australia is thus responsible for Papua (formerly British

New Guinea) and for the territory of New Guinea (formerly German), the latter under mandate. The two countries together form the eastern half of the great island of New Guinea, the western half of which was originally administered by the Dutch. Excluding Australia itself, New Guinea is the largest island in the world, its total area being about 235,000 square miles. It was the scene of a fiercely fought campaign with the Japanese in the Second World War. Australia also controls Norfolk and and other scattered islands and a wedge of Antarctic mainland territory.

New Zealand administers under mandate the territory of Western Samoa (formerly German) and she is also responsible for the Tokelau group of islands off Samoa and for the Ross dependency in the Antarctic. The Andaman and Nicobar islands belong to India. South Africa controls the mandated territory of South West Africa (formerly German), about 318,000 square miles in extent, but this has now become virtually an integral part of the Union. Canada has no dependencies, though she has close trading relations with the British West Indies.

Meanwhile, all the scattered Pacific islands come within the purview of the South Pacific Commission which was set up in 1947 to represent six powers then interested in the Pacific area, namely, Britain, Australia, New Zealand, France, Netherlands, and the United States, somewhat on the model of the Caribbean Commission. The Commission holds periodic conferences at some Pacific centre such as Suva in Fiji, to discuss problems and concert measures for dealing with matters of common interest in the area. It is obvious that many of these communities are too small and too weak economically to form viable independent units in the conditions of the modern world, and their future is therefore a Commonwealth problem.

Having completed our geographical survey, we must now consider some general questions of colonial administration, both at the centre and locally, and various problems affecting colonial territories as a whole.

CHAPTER VIII

THE CENTRAL MACHINERY

It is sometimes assumed or implied, not only in other countries but even in Britain, that the colonies are governed from Whitehall, but this is not the case. The broad lines of colonial policy are necessarily settled by the Colonial Office, since its political head is responsible to Parliament, and it offers expert advice and guidance, dispenses development and welfare funds voted by Parliament and determines matters concerned with the higher ranks of the Colonial Service; but the actual administration and financial control of the territories is the province of the Colonial Governments which have considerable discretion and scope in the exercise of their powers, and which as we shall see are in many instances being made increasingly responsible to the inhabitants of the colonies, with a view to eventual self-government. It has often been believed, moreover, and indeed is still believed in some quarters in America and elsewhere, that Britain taxes her colonies or derives some revenues from them. Absurd as it may seem, this belief or delusion applied even to what were lately called the Dominions, and some people in the United States believed that we taxed Canada or at least still held some power over that country. If such illusions exist in regard to the sovereign nations of the Commonwealth, their persistence in relation to the colonies is perhaps more understandable. Nevertheless, we do not as a country derive any revenue from the colonies (apart of course from profits on British undertakings there) but on the contrary, for many years past, the British people have contributed, and are still contributing, substantial sums towards their development.

In one sense of course Britain is still the centre of what used to be called the colonial empire, for so long as these countries or any of them remain under her authority or protection, the British people in the last analysis are responsible for their present and future well-being. This responsibility is exercised, on behalf of Parliament and the Cabinet, by the Secretary of State for the Colonies, and it is therefore necessary to examine the central machinery of colonial administration in London before dealing with the Colonial governments and the Colonial Service generally.

The principal departments in London concerned with the colonies are the Colonial Office itself, of which the Secretary of State is the political head, the Crown Agents for the Colonies, and the Colonial Audit Department. The latter departments, though separate, also come under the authority of the Secretary of State. The Department of Overseas Trade appoints representatives in various colonies and some Colonial governments appoint Commissioners or other representatives in this country. Grouped around the official departments or independent thereof are numerous advisory committees, institutions and voluntary bodies concerned wholly or in part with colonial affairs. Unlike other colonial powers, Britain maintains no general Colonial Council, although the Secretary of State has experts and special committees to advise him where necessary.

The Colonial Office can boast a fairly respectable antiquity, since it is the successor of earlier bodies which go back to 1660. In that year the Privy Council set up a "Committee for the Plentaçons" which blossomed out before the end of the year into a separate "Council of Foreign Plantations". Twelve years later, in 1672, this body was combined with the Council for Trade under the title of the "Council of Trade and Plantations". With one interval between 1677 and 1695 when, overcome by lethargy, it sank back into the parent Privy Council, the joint body continued in existence until 1782, the affairs of India being also committed to its charge in 1748. Shortly before its demise, however, an additional Secretary of State had been appointed in 1768 for the American Department, and the two authorities coexisted until they were both abolished in 1782 on the loss of the American colonies.

After a short interregnum, a new "Committee for Trade and Foreign Plantations" was organized in 1784, to which colonial affairs were for a time committed, but in 1794, for some strange reason, the Secretary for War also became nominally Secretary of State for the Colonies, and the Committee for

Trade and Plantations gradually ceased to have any connexion with colonial affairs and became the Board of Trade. The War and Colonial departments were formally united in 1801, but after the conclusion of the Napoleonic wars, the colonies became the principal concern of the Secretary of State, and in 1854 the War Department was finally separated from the Colonies. The India Office was at the same time organized under a separate Secretary of State.

From 1854, the organization of the Colonial Office continued to expand steadily but slowly until the First World War, when colonial policy began to assume its modern form. This was of course the culmination of a great change in the status of the self-governing colonies, which had now become Dominions, and this necessitated an entirely different handling of their relations with Great Britain. Their affairs were accordingly transferred to a new department carved out of the existing Colonial Office, and thus in 1925 the Dominions Office was set up, with a new Secretary of State at its head. For a time the two offices were held by the same Minister, but later this practice ceased and the offices were held by separate members of the Cabinet. Throughout this period the Secretary of State for India and his department remained quite distinct until their disappearance after India and Pakistan had become independent nations within the Commonwealth, when their relations with Great Britain, like those of the other equal partners with Britain in the Commonwealth were dealt with through the Commonwealth Relations Office, as the Dominions Office had by that time become.

The present Colonial Office therefore deals exclusively with the affairs of the territories described in this book, and as in course of time these in their turn attain full nationhood, their affairs, if they elect to remain within the Commonwealth, will naturally be transferred to the Commonwealth Relations Office, as has already happened in the case of Ceylon. For a special reason, Maltese affairs, as we have seen, may be transferred to the Home Office. It follows therefore that with the full implementation of our colonial policy the Colonial Office itself is destined like Balzac's *peau de chagrin* to shrink until eventually it should merge with the department to which it gave birth in 1925, the present Commonwealth Relations Office. But is is precisely during its present crucial period that by far its most important task remains to be accomplished and the Office which originated with the seventeenth-century committee finally fulfils its function in the transition from empire into free commonwealth.

As with other government departments, the Secretary of State is assisted by a Parliamentary Secretary, and of late years, owing to the great increase in the complexity and burden of the work, a Minister of State has also been appointed. The Secretary of State is usually a member of the Cabinet, and it has been the rule to arrange that one minister should sit in the Commons and the other, usually the junior, in the Lords, although this depends upon the balance of members of the government as between the two Houses. Whilst political chiefs naturally change with the government, there has been an increasing tendency in recent years to regard the broad lines of colonial policy as beyond party politics, and for that policy to continue to be applied without very material change irrespective of the party in power. The opposition naturally exercises its full rights of criticism, but though its tempo may vary mainly with the pressure of events, the declared objects of our colonial policy remain unchanged.

The organization of the Colonial Office is generally similar to other executive departments of State, but unlike the others, which for the most part deal with particular functions of government, such as foreign or home affairs, education, health, trade, etc., the Colonial Office has always been virtually an *imperium in imperio*, for it has to concern itself with every aspect of colonial administration as a whole. The civil service head of the office is the Permanent Under Secretary of State, who is assisted by two deputies and several assistant under secretaries in charge of departments.

Apart from the expert advisory, research and other special staffs, the office is organized in departments covering all the colonies in geographical groups, certain subject departments and a personnel division, covering recruitment and the Colonial Service. The subject divisions include African studies, economics, defence, international relations, communications, social services and welfare, besides the more usual administrative matters, such as finance, establishment, information and library, legal, registry, statistics and supplies. The expert advisory staff deal with all matters relating to agriculture, animal health, co-operation, education, fisheries, forestry, inland transport, labour, legal questions, medicine, mineral resources, social welfare and surveys. There is a strong research division, to which are attached the heads of various special committees and bureaux and the directors of colonial surveys.

Besides the individual advisers to the Secretary of State, the Colonial Office draws upon a wide fund of special knowledge through the membership of a number of advisory committees, such as those on colonial colleges, colonial geology and mineral resources, co-operation, education, the council on agriculture, animal health and forestry, education, the medical and sanitary committee, the economic and development council, civil aviation, economic research, fisheries, insecticides, and tsetse-fly committee, labour, land tenure, local government and native law panels, medical research, products, social science and general research councils, mass education and community development, university grants, and other special bodies which vary as the needs arise. The Office has been more than once reorganized the better to deal with its many and changing functions, and no doubt further reorganization will be necessary as the colonial territories and problems progressively develop in the future.

Special interest attaches to its control of development funds. In earlier days it was considered that colonies were in general entitled only to such expenditure as could be met or guaranteed from their own resources, but this was obviously a severe handicap to the poorer and less advanced countries, and undoubtedly led in many cases to comparative neglect and lack of progress. About the time of the First World War, this strict doctrine had begun to give way to a more generous conception of our colonial responsibility, and force was lent to this in particular by the case of the West Indies which had suffered greatly by the fall in world prices of their staple industry of sugar.

The first Development and Welfare Act reached the statute book in 1929 and special provision, as we have seen, was made for the West Indies. This Act was followed by two later Acts in 1940 and 1945, and up to 1952 over £140,000,000 had been voted by Parliament for development and welfare expenditure throughout the colonies. In addition to this the Colonial Development Corporation was set up with an initial capital of £100,000,000 to support or sponsor schemes likely to be commercially justified. From all these sources aided by local funds, a total expenditure was envisaged in 1952 of over £456,000,000 under development plans throughout the colonies, and many further plans have been sanctioned since that date.

The procedure has been broadly to ask every Colonial Government to prepare plans for the developments in their view most needed locally and to examine and co-ordinate these plans with expert assistance in London. Expenditure is sanctioned subject to the financial position and in accordance with an agreed order of priority, non-commercial schemes being considered by the Colonial Economic and Development Council or other appropriate body amongst those already indicated, and commercial schemes coming within the purview of the Colonial Development Corporation. Research into every aspect of colonial development and welfare is constantly proceeding both in London and in the colonies and forms the background to all this effort.

Various other special activities of the Colonial Office will be referred to when we come to consider colonial policy and problems. Public interest in and responsibility for colonial affairs is manifested through Parliament, which can call the Government or the Colonial Secretary to account through a debate on any particular colonial question, or through the annual debate on the estimates, or by questions to Ministers. In these days, colonial questions tend to occupy increasing space in the Press, and public interest is expressed not only through societies and other bodies concerned with the Commonwealth at home but to a growing extent by peoples and parties in the colonies themselves. Thus the Colonial Office and the Government are subjected to the pressure of public opinion (not always unfortunately adequately informed) and this interest is reflected in the political parties, who each maintain committees of members interested in colonial affairs.

There is however scope for a non-party or bipartisan Parliamentary Joint Committee on Colonial Affairs, to which both Lords and Commons would contribute their best-informed members. For the investigation of particular questions from time to time a Parliamentary committee or departmental commission, or in the case of important issues, a Royal Commission may be appointed. Before the Second World War, periodic Colonial Conferences were held, but these have been superceded in the growing pace of events by constant consultations at home and visits to the colonies. Nevertheless there might still be room for an occasional full-dress Conference in London of colonial representatives or of some form of standing Colonial Advisory Council.

To an increasing extent in this air age, the Secretary of State and his deputy Ministers are peripatetic and have constant opportunities of first-hand contacts with colonial peoples and problems, which is certainly an improvement on earlier days when a Secretary of State might have little personal knowledge of the colonies for which he was responsible. Individuals or groups of members of Parliament also visit the colonies from time to time, and there is a growing interchange of members of the Colonial Office staff and of the Colonial Service, which is all to the good.

Besides the Colonial Office, there is another department in London, equally under the authority of the Secretary of State, though separate from the Colonial Office, which stands in a fiduciary relation to both and acts as a link between the two, and that is the office of the Crown Agents.

The three Crown Agents at the head of this office are appointed by the Secretary of State, but their department acts not for the British Government but directly for the individual Colonial Governments and for various colonial municipal, harbour and other public authorities besides. The expenses of the department are borne proportionately by those for whom it acts, the rates of commission charged for these services being fixed by the Secretary of State, who is also generally responsible for the staff. The arrangement is therefore in a sense triangular, but it functions very well. The Crown Agents carry out all the business contracts, technical work and financial operations of some sixty Governments and other public authorities, and the office is housed in a spacious building at Millbank near the Houses of Parliament and also maintains a branch in the City. In a single year, stores and machinery totalling over £15,000,000 in value may be purchased, tested and shipped overseas, and more than 500,000 tons of cargo are normally handled in the same period. Moreover, colonial loans amounting to considerably over £100,000,000 are administered by the department, and many other functions are carried out.

As the present efficient system is the result of a process of gradual evolution and change extending over more than a century, it may be of interest to glance at the history of the department and to examine its present organization in some detail. In early days individual colonies maintained their own purchasing and contract agents in London, and these often acted as political and general agents also, but in those days the colonies included the now independent members of the Commonwealth. Communications were then a matter of slow sailing voyages, irregular and frequently interrupted. As a result, the Home Government possessed but limited control over these distant settlements, and the rulers of the outposts enjoyed a considerable measure of freedom of action. "John Company" of course looked after its own business, but the Governors of the other colonies appointed their own agents, some of whom were almost ambassadors in their duties. Later however the Secretary of State gained further control, and although formally appointed by the Governor, the agents were nominated at home and their duties restricted purely to commercial matters.

For the most part, however, these agents continued to act independently of each other and to build up their own methods of business and impose their own requirements irrespective of what was being done elsewhere. Moreover, the purchases of single colonies were relatively small and they competed more or less in the same markets. As the colonies developed and important public works and railways were undertaken, the consequences of this lack of system and uniformity became increasingly serious. Railways were built to different gauges, specifications for locomotives, plant and mechanical parts were almost as numerous as the different contracts, which of course meant unnecessarily heavy costs, different consulting engineers were employed, each with their own standards, and purchases of stores were erratic and uneconomical. This state of things soon brought about "frequent and grave complaints" by the Colonial Governments and the Home Government intervened.

After a searching inquiry, a consolidated agency was established in 1833, under the title of the Agents General for the Crown Colonies, and from that year onwards things began to improve. As the self-governing colonies (later the Dominions) developed, they established their own Agents General here, but meanwhile the Colonial Empire greatly expanded, and eventually the department became the Crown Agents for the Colonies, now for oversea territories and administrations.

Broadly speaking the work of the department today may be grouped into finance, appointments and pensions, stores and general supplies, engineering designs and contracts, shipping and insurance, and certain miscellaneous services. All loans raised and other financial operations by Colonial Governments and other public authorities are handled in this country by the Crown Agents. Appointments for the main branches of the Colonial Service are of course made by the Colonial Office, but a great many technical and subsidiary posts are filled by the Crown Agents acting on behalf of the individual Colonial Governments. They include all varieties of staff for railways and public works and surveys, accounting, marine, printing, wireless, motor, sanitary and other services and police appointments. Many a career spent in distant parts of the world has started with an interview on Millbank. The Crown Agents also pay salaries of officers on leave and pensions on retirement.

But the great bulk of the Crown Agents' work is concerned with engineering contracts, designs and technical consulting work, with the ordering of supplies of all kinds, their inspecting and testing, and their shipment overseas. The Crown Agents supply everything from bridges to drawing-pins. They may have to undertake the clothing and equipment of a colonial regiment or the construction of a railway extension, or at the other end of the scale they may receive an indent for a few buttons or a bag of nails, though of course certain supplies of trifling amount are purchased on the spot to the benefit of local trade. Naturally there is a long-standing controversy in some colonies on this point, but on the whole it has been found more efficient and economical to order most supplies through the Crown Agents. The result of long experience has shown that this system of ordering everything through one centre with expert staffs and high standards, is on the whole, though by no means free from defects, better on balance than any practical alternative. Nobody would now advocate returning to the old unregulated individual way, but the effect of the changing status of many of the colonies must be considered in this connexion.

The Crown Agents are however much more than mere purchasing and shipping agents. They have generally brought order and simplicity into a wide engineering field where confusion once reigned, where every locomotive was an original design with its own special parts only to be obtained in one quarter, manufactured and stocked for the purpose and charged accordingly, and on top of this, having to be approved by a particular consulting engineer. The Crown Agents have now built up a complete and simplified system of standards covering railways, rolling stock, bridges and so forth down to the smallest replacement. They have worked out designs for a great variety of conditions, so that it is now possible, for instance, to send a telegram home giving certain letters and numbers and a complete bridge will be shipped with every bolt and nut to be erected in position. The technical staff of the Crown Agents are always ready to give skilled advice on every subject coming within their province. Duplicates of all drawings and designs are kept at Millbank and indexed so that it is never necessary to pass these to and fro, with consequent delay, but only to give the reference number. In all this, the Crown Agents have of course been aided by the movement towards standardization in engineering and industry generally represented by the British Standards Institution, and indeed have played their own part in that movement.

Another important service rendered by the Crown Agents is the rigorous and expert testing, often at the manufacturers' own works, of all classes of goods supplied, from steel girders to uniforms. It is obvious that the knowledge required to test and pass the many hundreds of supplies that pass through the Crown Agents' hands calls for a wide range of craftsmanship, for apart from engineering and machinery of all kinds, there may be medical supplies, boots, tents, small-arms, tropical kit, scientific apparatus, petrol, cement, paint, china, glass and cutlery, stationery and printing, coal, furniture, and even statuary, pedigree livestock, street decorations and fireworks!

One function that will appeal to philatelists all over the world is the design and printing of postage stamps for all Colonial Governments for both regular and special issues. Great care and secrecy has to be exercised over every stage of this work, preparation of designs, making and issue of special water-marked paper, and especially meticulous scrutiny to detect any defects, for "freak" stamps which escape into circulation acquire great philatelic value. Quite an appreciable revenue accrues to colonial funds from the stamp trade and mutual benefits result from the arrangement whereby the Office acts as intermediary for the sale of stamps.

The Crown Agents also undertake the sale in this country of all Colonial Government publications, of which there is a wide range. The various Colonial Currency Boards are housed at Millbank, and the Office undertakes the supply of coin to all colonies that have not their own currency boards. Many other miscellaneous duties also fall to its share, as for instance the arranging of passages of colonial officials, their wives and families, and of special missions by sea and air to every quarter of the globe. One Crown Agent also looks after colonial students sent with private resources to study in this country, although most colonial students here are the charge of the Colonial Office, as we shall see under Education later.

Notwithstanding the multifarious duties which they thus perform, the cost of these services to the Colonial Governments, if worked out at a flat rate of the whole turnover annually, forms only a fractional percentage of the total, and it is safe to say that, taking everything into account, with the accumulated tradition and experience of the Office, the same result could not be achieved with equal security, efficiency and economy in any other way.

As the various colonies or groups develop into self-governing units, however, it is pertinent to speculate as to the future of the complex organization built up over a century and more to serve all these special needs. Many colonies may naturally wish to exercise full freedom in this matter, although Ceylon for example, after attaining independent status, did retain the Crown Agents services in many respects. Some authorities will doubtless always find these services both useful and economical, but it is permissible to hope that full scope will be found for such an efficient organization and its expert services for a very long time to come. (This now seems assured.)

Another department in London which may be briefly glanced at is the Colonial Audit. As it is desirable in the interests of financial efficiency that the task of auditing colonial accounts and expenditure should be carried out by an independent body, not in any way subject to those responsible for the expenditure, the Colonial Audit Department has a central office in London in charge of a Director under whom work all the audit officers in the colonies. They are responsible directly to him and not to the local government or to the Colonial Office. The Director renders his report to the Secretary of State, and the expenses are defrayed, as in the case of the Crown Agents, by the Governments affected, a trifling sum in each case. All these arrangements make for economy and financial integrity.

To look after colonial trade and British interests therein, the Overseas Trade department of the Board of Trade appoints Trade Commissioners in various colonies and groups, and in the smaller colonies officers of the local Government act as trade correspondents for the department, which under its own Minister does everything possible to foster trade between Great Britain and the colonies. Many colonies also maintain Commissioners or trade and information offices in London to look after their interests here. Valuable reports on colonial trade and industry are published by the department and by Colonial Governments, and these are reinforced by both annual and special reports and economic and statistical reports issued by the Colonial Office, to which reference is made in the bibliography.

In addition to the many special committees and other bodies already mentioned under the Colonial office, there are others in

London whose activities cover the Commonwealth as a whole, such as the Imperial Economic Committee, the Imperial Agricultural Bureaux, the Imperial Institute of Entomology, the Imperial Mycological Institute, the Imperial Forestry Institute and Conference, the Imperial Communications Advisory Committee, the London and Liverpool Schools of Hygiene and Tropical Medicine, the School of African and Oriental Studies, the Empire Cotton Growing Corporation, the Overseas Nursing Association, and other bodies. Doubtless the term Commonwealth will be substituted for Imperial in the titles of many of these bodies, and other changes may take place in course of time. Two institutions which deserve special mention are the Imperial or Commonwealth Institute in London and the Royal Botanic Gardens at Kew, for these carry out varied and valuable research work which also benefits the colonies generally. Kew is, of course, known throughout the world; amongst many other examples of its work for the colonies in the past have been its introduction of breadfruit into the West Indies, for which purpose Captain Bligh of the *Bounty* was commissioned, and the introduction of rubber into Malaya, and Ceylon. It trains botanists for work in the colonies and carries out much valuable research work in economic botany from day to day.

Although not in London but in Trinidad, the work of the Imperial College of Tropical Agriculture far transcends the geographical limits of the West Indies, and like the work of other research stations in the colonies, such as the Amani Institute in Tanganyika, its results are available to the colonies as a whole. Voluntary associations will be referred to later.

CHAPTER IX

COLONIAL GOVERNMENT AND SERVICE

SINCE the British colonial empire grew up in the past in all sorts of ways, there is naturally no uniformity to be found in the systems of government of individual colonies, and as they develop at varying paces and in different ways towards self-government, this will be even less so in the future. Nevertheless, colonial government has in general followed certain broad lines which can be described irrespective of variations in particular instances. This is the general form of administration loosely referred to as "crown colony government", though it also applies to protectorates and other territories. The term "Crown colony" was originally introduced to distinguish between the then self-governing colonies, later the Dominions, and the non-self-governing dependencies of the Crown, but the term is now virtually obsolete, Since protectorates are not technically part of British territory, they are judicially on a different basis, their peoples being "protected persons" and not British subjects; there is however often little difference in the form of administration.

The authority of the Crown is exercised through the Governor, who is the Royal representative. In some cases he is called the High Commissioner, and in Jamaica for example he is styled Captain-General, following old Spanish usage, but his authority and functions are virtually the same in all cases. The Governor is selected by the Secretary of State, usually from senior officers of the Colonial Service, though sometimes from outside, and he is appointed by the Crown. He receives his commission in the form of "Letters Patent" under the Great Seal, which are supplemented by "Instructions" under the Royal Sign Manual and Signet. These are terms going far back into English history, but in practice the Letters Patent and Instructions together form a sort of organic or basic law of the territory.

COLONIAL GOVERNMENT AND SERVICE

These instruments generally define the boundaries and status of the territory; empower and command the Governor to do all things proper to his office, after taking the prescribed form of oaths of allegiance and for the due execution of his office and the impartial administration of justice; define the composition, constitution and powers of executive and legislative councils; reserve power to the Crown to disallow ordinances and to legislate by Order in Council in emergencies; confer on the Governor the exercise of the prerogative of mercy; define the procedure of assent to or reservation of Bills; empower him to suspend public officers, to make provision for administration in his own absence, and so forth.

All Governors are assisted by executive councils, and the majority by legislative councils also, although in a few of the more primitive territories authority is exercised directly through the executive council. This body acts as a privy council and is normally composed of the chief public officers, such as the colonial secretary, the attorney-general, the treasurer, and possibly certain heads of departments, together with in most cases "unofficial" members prominent in or representative of the community and either nominated by the Governor or elected.

The legislative body, whatever may be its local title, varies in composition in different colonies, and in pursuance of the general policy of progress towards self-government, colonial constitutions are from time to time revised in the direction of greater liberality and enlargement of the franchise. In certain of the West Indian colonies, the legislatures date from as far back as the sixteenth century and have their own distinctive features. In both the Bahamas and Barbados the legislative body has two chambers, namely the legislative council and house of assembly, and in Barbados originally a sort of buffer was interposed between the two in the shape of an executive committee. This device was due to Sir Conrad Reeves, a distinguished African who was Chief Justice of the colony, and in practice it greatly improved the working of the constitution. All these forms however give way in time to full democratic responsible government, for it is a merit of the Crown colony system that it can be progressively modified until it issues in complete self-government.

Even where the ordinary form of Crown colony government functions, however, a wise Governor never fails in practice to consult the general feeling of the community either directly or through the nominated or elected members; and even officials do not always confine themselves to registering an official vote, but often express independent views in the true interests of the community. In the background, there is always the watchful eye of the Secretary of State and his staff in London, who is of course always subject to the pressure of public opinion at home exerted through Parliament and the Press. Not infrequently, whatever the precise form of government, it has turned out that "what is best administered is best". That is not to say, of course, that there are not many imperfections in colonial as in other forms of government, but the whole structure is flexible and can be adapted to changing circumstances up to the attainment of full independence.

Before passing on to the organic structure of government, it is desirable here to glance at the operation of Indirect Rule or Native Administration, although further reference will be made to this subject later. In various territories, especially in tropical Africa, native or tribal institutions were found to be functioning fairly satisfactorily. This was the case, for example, in some of the Hausa states in Nigeria, in certain areas of the Gold Coast and Ashanti, in the kingdom of the Buganda in Uganda, in Basutoland, and to take quite a different example, in the Malay states. Both for reasons of expediency and economy in administration, and later as a deliberate policy with constructive aim, it was decided, particularly in Africa, to continue these indigenous institutions in being, though in some cases certain features repugnant to civilized ideas had to be corrected, gradually to improve and strengthen them, and as far as possible to work through them, so that the people might eventually have the form of government best suited to their peculiar genius. In many cases, these Native Administrations have been successfully incorporated in the larger entity of a central government.

This system of indirect rule owed much to Lord Lugard and Sir George Goldie and to Sir Donald Cameron among others. It has many obvious advantages and certain drawbacks

COLONIAL GOVERNMENT AND SERVICE 129

which will be discussed later. But in the result many African peoples have continued to live under institutions familiar to them, and Native Administrations enjoy considerable autonomy in the conduct of their own affairs, having their own treasuries and public services, administering justice, collecting their own revenues and so forth, with the advice and assistance of British officers. Thus, to cite but a few examples at random, the Sardauna of Sokoto, the Alake of Abeokuta, the Asantehene of Ashanti, and the Kabaka of Buganda rule over their own territories. There are further examples in Bechuanaland and other African territories and there are of course many native states under our protection with British Residents in Malaya, Zanzibar, and elsewhere, as well as those instances where native assemblies have their place in the structure of government, like the great council of chiefs in Fiji. There has indeed been room and opportunity for the operation and development of every form of government in the British colonial system.

Turning now to the normal structure of the administration, the principal officer next to the Governor is the Colonial Secretary, who presides over the secretariat and normally administers the government in the Governor's absence. The secretariat is the central administrative office of the colony, and the Colonial Secretary is usually an officer of wide experience who may normally expect promotion to a Governorship. His office is the regular channel of approach to the Governor, and it also coordinates the activities of the other departments. It may be noted here that "Colonial Regulations", a lengthy code of rules dealing with matters of appointments, discipline, salaries, leave, precedence, correspondence, etc., provide that every individual in a colony has the right to address or petition the Secretary of State in London, but he must forward his communication through the Governor, who is bound to transmit it, accompanied by his report or observations.

The principal departments in a colony may be classified as administrative, legal, financial, social and technical, varying in number and complexity with the size, importance and development of the particular territory. The judiciary is headed by a Chief Justice, with puisne judges and magistrates, and often there are native courts also whose jurisdiction is defined. Appeal usually lies to the Supreme or High Court of the colony with recourse in certain cases to London. There can of course be no doubt as to the impartiality and integrity of the justice administered in any British territory, but there may be some doubt as to whether, by the nature of their appointment, colonial legal officers can be in all circumstances as completely independent of the executive or of the Colonial Office as are the judiciary in this country. The legal side is represented by the Attorney-General and sometimes also by a Solicitor-General and Crown counsel, and there is usually ample scope in the judicial and legal branches for indigenous talent. It may also be remarked that in many colonies, especially in Africa, the people seem to display a decided taste for litigation. Police and prisons branches also of course come under this department.

If there is a provincial or regional organization, it is normally headed by Provincial or District Commissioners, but the backbone of all British colonial administration is the District Officer, who has to discharge almost every civil function in the often large area over which he practically rules, and in primitive communities is father and mother to his community. Chiefs and headmen and village councils act under his supervision.

The financial branches include the Treasury, the Customs (from which the main colonial revenues are often drawn) and the accounts of the independent Audit. Other usual colonial departments are medical and public health, education, agriculture, public works, railways (generally state-owned in the colonies), posts and telegraphs, land and surveys, perhaps mines, forestry and so forth. The defence force will be under a commanding officer or officers and it must be remembered that the Governor is always Commander-in-Chief. The organization of each colony is given in the annual Colonial Office List. Further information as to the working of all the organs of government in the colonies will be found in the books by Sir Anton Bertram on *The Colonial Service* and by Sir Charles Jeffries on *The Colonial Empire and its Civil Service*, but while much in them is still applicable today, it must be remembered that both organization and service are changing all the time.

The Colonial Service

Turning now to the Colonial Service itself, this well deserves comparison with those other great bodies, the Home and Indian civil services and the Sudan political service, of all of which Britons may justifiably be proud, for they have given a high example to the world. Only the Home and Colonial services now remain, and the Colonial service, though much younger than the others, has built up a corporate tradition and practice second to none, and fully adequate to the performance of its immensely important and responsible task.

Yet it is only within comparatively recent years that it has become unified into a single Service. In earlier days, of course, the various colonial services included those of what are now the independent nations of the Commonwealth, but we are concerned here only with the present colonies. Like his predecessor, the junior "collector" in the early days of British India, the young assistant district officer in the colonies may have many and varied responsibilities for the community under his charge, with the important difference however that communications and methods have vastly changed since early days in India, and the colonial officer today is always in close touch with superior authority. This may not necessarily lessen the difficulty of his task. There is in fact no finer field for the talents of youth, no better scope for the development of character and the qualities of decision, judgement and leadership, no more worthwhile career than is offered by the Colonial Service today and will so continue for many years to come.

At first each colony recruited its own civil service on its own conditions, appointments being entirely in the hands of the Governor. The great bulk of the minor posts are still recruited locally, but for the more responsible of these the Governor makes provisional appointments which must be reported for the Secretary of State's confirmation, which in practice is usually forthcoming. Selection for posts above the minor executive grades, and for all posts within what are now the "unified" as distinguished from local services, rests with the Secretary of State. The term "selection" is used advisedly, for although the Secretary of State, through the Colonial Service Appointments

Board, selects officers for the Service, the appointment to the actual post is made by the Governor. The Colonial Service today comprises in all somewhere about 250,000 men and women, but only 10,000 of these are in the "unified" branches, the members of which are selected at home, the others being recruited locally.

From early days when the choice of men to assist him in his task of ruling a colony was left to the Governor, the Colonial Office gradually began to gain more control over the selection of men for the higher or special posts. Even when candidates were chosen chiefly on personal grounds or were the subject of ministerial patronage, the Colonial Office managed to introduce some measure of uniformity in regard to qualifications, pay and conditions of work, subject to local differences.

After the First World War, when many special problems had to be dealt with in the colonial field, it became necessary to strengthen the organization at headquarters for the recruitment and training of candidates. In 1927 the first Colonial Office Conference studied the problem especially in relation to the requirements of scientific posts for which special training was needed. Later a wider organization, the Warren Fisher Committee, was appointed to consider the Colonial Service as a whole, and the report of this Committee, which was adopted by the 1930 Conference, led to the present system of unification. The Committee dealt with every aspect of the Service, including recruitment, status, pay, conditions, leave, pensions and so forth, and in the result unified administrative, legal, medical, agricultural, veterinary and forestry services were set up, and other branches were added later.

The Secretary of State emphasized at the time that unification did not mean uniformity. The primary objects of the change were to raise the standards of the Colonial Service, to provide a career worthy in its opportunities and its rewards of the best talents from the Home country and the Dominions, and to an increasing extent from the colonies themselves, and to offer to all the colonies, the smallest and poorest equally with the larger and more prosperous, a choice of the best human material for their service, such as many of them could not secure otherwise. The fact that the world-wide colonial field is open to candidates entering the unified Colonial Service makes it possible to attract the best men and women for the purpose.

At the Colonial Office itself a strong organization exists in the Personnel Division concerned with recruitment, training and establishment matters. The primary duty of the Recruitment department is to find suitable candidates for the Service and to present them for selection to the Appointments Board, a body consisting of Civil Service Commissioners and other specialists, upon whose recommendation the Secretary of States nominates to the Service. The department is in contact with the universities and other agencies and with the general public, and does all the preliminary work including interviews prior to the decision of the Board. A high standard of general education is essential; though a university degree is not absolutely indispensable, candidates selected in recent years have nearly all been in possession of a degree, usually with honours.

In former years candidates for what were then the Eastern Cadet services had to undergo a stiff competitive examination, but the Warren Fisher Committee reported that the balance of advantage lay in favour of stringent measures of selection, with safeguards of course in regard to standards of education, for the Colonial Service required something more than ability to pass an examination. Character and judgement are also necessary, and even when the Board has formed its opinion on all the evidence available, including of course a personal interview, successful candidates are only appointed at first on probation. Latterly the gathering together of selected candidates in a country-house setting for observation of testing of personal qualities has also been tried. On probation, they are given special courses at Oxford and Cambridge in subjects including anthropology, native languages, law and colonial history, the results of which are tested by examination, and a certain standard must be reached before actual nomination.

After successfully passing these courses, selected candidates are assigned to the colonies in which vacancies exist, regard being paid as far as practicable to individual preferences. Scholarships are also available in special branches, and this, as well as the holding of "refresher" courses for serving officers, is also the business of the Recruitment and Training department. For the first few years, the young officer (not being a specialist) is generally employed in district administration; later may come periods of attachment to the secretariat or other colonial departments, or even perhaps to the Colonial Office in London, officers of which are also transferred from time to time for service in the colonies. For the information of the public, there is a useful Colonial Office pamphlet compiled by Kenneth Bradley, *The Colonial Service as a Career*.

The unification of the Service does not imply that intercolonial transfer is the lot of every officer, or even of the majority. Generally speaking, the colonies which employ large staffs provide within their own borders a satisfactory career, while for many of the higher posts local knowledge and experience are essential. At the same time there is in the unified service a considerable number of administrative and other posts filled by selection from the Service as a whole. This is where the Colonial Service department at the Colonial Office comes in, for it keeps personal records of all officers serving, including confidential reports from the Governor of each territory, and notes of the officers' own wishes as to the work or colony they prefer. These reports are studied as the basis of lists available for consideration in connexion with vacancies, promotions, etc. This department also deals with regulations and conditions of employment, leave, pensions and so forth throughout the Service.

While the junior officer may in any case fairly look forward in due course to doing responsible work in his own territory, he may also legitimately feel that he carries a Colonial Secretary's pen or even a Governor's cocked hat in his knapsack. In the higher appointments indeed there has been some criticism that officers who have become thoroughly familiar with one territory are then transferred to a quite different one and so in a sense have to start all over again in a strange environment, but this is the other side of having a larger field of talent to select from and wider opportunities of promotion. Such an officer often returns to his earlier environment in a superior position. Similar criticism has been applied to Governors appointed to another colony just when their work is beginning to bear fruit, which it is thought may have a stultifying effect, but the alternative might be stagnation and a consequent lowering of standards. The interests of the territory should be paramount, but these interests undoubtedly include a first-class Colonial Service.

Members of the local service, usually inhabitants of the colony, are by no means debarred from entry into the unified service; indeed every encouragement is given them, and it is the general policy to encourage native-born people of whatever race to enter the service of their country and gradually to fill more and more of the higher posts. It should here be recalled that many specialist appointments are made not by the Colonial Office but, as we have seen, by the Crown Agents.

Brief reference should be made here to the defence forces of the colonies. Most colonies raise and maintain their own troops and are responsible for the local defence; such stations as Gibraltar and Malta, and to some extent Aden and Singapore, are in a special category. Amongst other famous colonial forces may be mentioned the West India Regiment, those well-known African Corps, the King's African Rifles, and the Royal West African Frontier Force, the Malay Regiment and similar corps in others colonies. The Colonial Office has a small Defence department of its own to co-ordinate these activities.

With its fine record in the past, the Colonial Service was never at a more severe testing-time than it is today. It is precisely in this critical transitional period, when colonies are emerging into independent peoples, that the highest qualities will be required of the public services. This period is likely to last for a long time yet, and it is vital that the best talent of all races should be recruited to those services. In the Sudan, the Gold Coast and Nigeria, to name only three countries, an incalculable debt is due to the wise guidance, restraint and unselfish devotion of their civil servants who had such a difficult task to fulfil and whose interests and future were rightly safeguarded in the transition from dependency to nation, and we shall need many more men and women of the same high calibre in the future.

It is indeed suggested that the present Colonial Service should be broadened into a Commonwealth Civil Service open to young peoples of all races and to specialists and technicians (of whom even more will be needed in the future) throughout the Commonwealth, and that Commonwealth Governments should be represented on the controlling body. This would be in line with the idea that the responsibility so long exercised by Great Britain alone for the future of all these peoples should be shared in some measure by other nations of the Commonwealth. (It is now to be known as the Overseas Service.)

It is appropriate that, after dealing with Service matters, we should remind ourselves of the outstanding part which the personal element has played in our colonial past. Whilst the British colonial empire, like Topsy, undoubtedly "growed" rather than was planned, it is not to be supposed that it did so without active and indeed decisive human agency. Less than any other colonial system was it the result of abstract Government action or policy, but rather the creation of a succession of enterprising, far-sighted and for the most part public-spirited individuals, missionaries, explorers, soldiers, administrators, even businessmen and traders, who compelled recognition and eventual support for their pioneer efforts upon a reluctant Home government. Necessarily the achievements of many of these pioneers belong to the Commonwealth as a whole, but the achievements of many of them were exercised largely in the present colonial sphere.

To anyone undertaking a study of the history of the British colonies, and few more fascinating subjects can be imagined, it would be both illuminating and rewarding to read not only the more impersonal works listed in the Bibliography, but also the lives of those outstanding personalities whose careers have exercised such a decisive influence upon British colonial history. They begin in the earliest days, and no complete catalogue can be attempted here, but it may suffice to name a few of the better known in different spheres of action. Among the great names are undoubtedly Stamford Raffles, Captain Cook, David Livingstone, Cecil Rhodes, Lord Lugard, Mungo Park, McGregor Laird, Mary Kingsley, Sir George Goldie, Sir John Kirk, outstanding colonial governors like Sir Gordon Guggisberg, Sir Hugh Clifford, Sir Donald Cameron and others, Sir James Brooke, Dr. Aggrey, to name only a few. In the

Caribbean there were the Warners and Codringtons, picturesque personalities like Sir Henry Morgan, buccaneer turned colonial governor, and indeed throughout the colonies from the West Indies to the South Seas many names stand out in the long record, but behind all are the many obscure and unknown individuals, traders, merchants, civil servants and others, whose patient and anonymous labours helped to build up the British colonial heritage and trust.

Moreover, as in every British sphere of action, voluntary effort and organization has played its essential part, and as we have already mentioned official bodies and committees, the tale may be completed with the voluntary societies.

The leading society in this field is the Royal Empire Society, which was founded in 1868 as the Colonial Society and later became the Royal Colonial Institute. Mention should be made of its excellent library, for this collection, with the Colonial Office Library, form the two chief depositories of Commonwealth records and literature. In this connexion reference should also be made to the Royal Institute of International Affairs, especially for its valuable studies and publications on Commonwealth subjects. The Overseas League, founded during the First World War by Sir Evelyn Wrench, who also founded the English-speaking Union, has headquarters in London and branches throughout the Commonwealth. The Royal African Society, as its name implies, is concerned with the affairs of the African continent, mainly though not exclusively those of British African territories. It was originally founded in memory of that remarkable woman, Mary Kingsley. A more specialized body is the International Institute of African Languages and Cultures, and Brussels is the headquarters of an International Colonial Institute.

Amongst other British societies is the Victoria League, and several of the "empire" societies have combined to form a joint Hospitality Committee which to some extent co-ordinates social functions. There are also bodies concerned with particular territories such as the Association of British Malaya, the West Indies Club and the West India Committee, a voluntary organization formed originally in 1750 to look after the economic and other interests of the West Indian colonies and merchants. The Corona Club was founded in the Colonial Office by Joseph Chamberlain and its membership is strictly confined to the Colonial Service. There are various colonial student societies in London and hostels such as London House, Aggrey House, etc., but these will be mentioned under Education in the following chapter.

Most of these bodies naturally had their origin during the developing period of the British Empire in the nineteenth century, and although some are adapting themselves to the new conditions, it would seem that there is room for a Commonwealth movement among all the peoples of that world-wide community, including the emergent countries, which would reflect the spirit of the Commonwealth today and express and promote more fully the ideals that bind us all together.

CHAPTER X

COLONIAL POLICY AND PROBLEMS

THE British colonial policy of trusteeship, with its declared objective of fitting the colonial peoples for eventual self-government, antedated the League of Nations, and marked out Britain in those early days as unique among colonial powers. Even before the provision for mandates under the League, which indeed owed its inspiration to the British example, we had fully accepted the implications of trusteeship not only for mandated territories but for all our colonies, and we were also the first to place our mandates under the Trusteeship Council of the United Nations.

Colonial self-government was never contemplated by the other colonial powers, and only the upsurge of nationalism after the Second World War has radically altered the scene, especially for the Dutch and French in Asia. So far the Belgian and Portuguese territories in Africa seem relatively unaffected, but the ferment in Africa will probably spread to all colonial territories in time. Belgium concentrates on economic well-being rather than political objectives, and in French Union territories in Africa the traditional French policy has been to concentrate on the elite and to endeavour to turn them into good Frenchmen, with representation in the French Parliament (where however they are necessarily in a small minority) rather than to encourage them to be good Africans and to lead their own countries into self-government and independence. Events it is true have determined otherwise in Asia. Under their pressure the Netherlands Indies were declared autonomous and united with Holland only under the Dutch Crown, but Indonesia is now independent, and the three territories of French Indo-China, Vietnam, Laos and Cambodia, though still within the Union, have had to be accorded a self-governing status. In Africa, as we have seen, all the colonial powers now co-operate closely together, but British colonial policy still remains distinct in its explicit aims.

Britain has throughout willed both the end and the means. Her present colonial policy is indeed but the logical and natural outcome of the progressive evolution of the former British Empire into a Commonwealth of equal nations. That evolution culminated with the supreme act of the attainment of full self-government in the Indian sub-continent (an act unique in history) and the subsequent free election of India and Pakistan to remain within the Commonwealth, which was also the choice of Ceylon, and although Burma decided to go outside, as she was fully entitled to do, she still maintains cordial relations with Britain and the Commonwealth. These developments followed in natural succession to the attainment of equal nationhood in the Commonwealth by the white Dominions, and pointed to the logical continuance of this process in British colonial policy.

We are therefore witnessing now the later stages in a more or less continuous process of natural evolution and growth, but undoubtedly this process has been accelerated since the Second World War by the rise of nationalism, in the British colonial sphere as elsewhere, among the politically backward peoples of the world, independently of whatever influence communism may have had in certain countries. What should be noted, however, by the student is that the whole trend of British political ideas and practice as applied to the colonies has been to encourage and foster the rise of a movement for political freedom on the same lines as the examples already set before them in Britain and the other Commonwealth nations. But while this development was in any case to be expected, wider events, and especially the effects of two world wars between the Western nations, have greatly accelerated the pace, and unless this can be in some measure controlled, and wisdom and restraint exercised on all sides, especially by the colonial peoples themselves, it may result in harm being done to their true long-term interests. That is why this transitional period is of crucial significance in the successful evolution of the emergent Commonwealth. So far, however, we have encouraging examples in the Gold Coast and Nigeria, and also in the initial stages of federation in Central Africa, and we may reasonably anticipate similar developments elsewhere.

Colonial self-government will not necessarily follow in all cases the model of British parliamentary insitutions, though it must be admitted that, perhaps naturally, this has been the ideal preferred and indeed demanded by the colonial peoples so far. For us it has developed out of a long process of historic evolution, and implies a certain background which may not exist in other communities, and whilst it certainly seems to have struck surprising roots in quite different soil, it must not be expected that it can show the same stability and results in a decade or two that have been painfully reached, and even now imperfectly, only over very many generations in Europe. That is why we have always taken care to cherish and where possible to strengthen and at the same time to adapt progressively to modern conditions such native institutions as we have found already in existence. This is the only true justification of "Indirect Rule". The genius of a people may be best expressed in its indigenous institutions, and with many primitive peoples, these may show a better way than the adoption or imposition of alien forms of government. Possibly in Africa and elsewhere, the best features of both can be preserved with European guidance allied to wise native leadership.

Not only Britain but the Commonwealth at large and the advanced nations generally have their responsibility towards the less politically developed peoples of the world. This is indeed recognized in the charter of the United Nations, but unfortunately as yet is but little implemented in practice. Under the League of Nations, the Permanent Mandates Commission, despite certain defects, accomplished much useful work and certainly proved a much more reasonable and practical body than its successor, the Trusteeship Council of the United Nations. That is because its members were experts in the colonial field—Lord Lugard for example was the British representative—and spent little time on abstract and sterile political issues. Even the Trusteeship Council, however, has a better record than the egregious 'Fourth Committee' which endeavoured to arrogate to itself vague and undefined powers over all colonial territories, but which only succeeded in turning itself into a sounding-board for uninformed political propaganda on the part of countries entirely without experience in the colonial field, and many of which would have been better occupied in setting their own house in order.

On paper the United Nations organization has devised a charter of rights for colonial peoples, admirable in sentiment, but in practice it has been the responsibility of the colonial powers, and especially Britain, to carry it into effect. We have always readily furnished any information in reason which has been demanded in respect of any of our colonial territories, in addition to those placed under the scrutiny of the Trusteeship Council, and indeed such information is available to all; but the responsibility for our colonial administration cannot be shared with others. This is a distinction dating even from League of Nations days that, whilst we freely recognize the right of a duly authorized international body both to information and to certain powers of supervision and criticism of our colonial administration, the actual administration itself cannot be shared, and indeed any attempt at divided or multiple responsibility (as even condominiums have shown) is foredoomed to failure and could never be in the interests of the colonial peoples themselves.

Apart from administration, however, which must remain the responsibility of the colonial power until its stewardship is brought to an end, much can be done in the international sphere to help the emergent peoples. Following up the precedent set by Britain in its development and welfare programme for all its colonial territories, already referred to under the Colonial Office in a previous chapter, the Colombo Plan was inaugurated at a meeting of Commonwealth ministers held in Ceylon, and this has been supplemented by funds made available by the Point Four programme of the United States for the assistance of under-developed countries. The Colombo Plan and the Point Four programme are not directed specifically towards British colonial territories, but are available to any countries which need such aid, and have been applied to countries like India and Pakistan and to many countries in Asia. In particular, the Colombo Plan provides not only funds for needed development but especially expert advice and the services of technicians of all kinds to carry out the actual work in the beneficiary countries. So far it has made good progress, but much more remains to be done.

Meanwhile the development and welfare programme of the British Government continues its beneficient activities, with of course the co-operation of the Colonial Governments themselves. In our geographical survey, we have mentioned some of the outstanding schemes sponsored by this agency. In addition to the funds allocated by the Colonial Development Advisory Council, there are the more commercial schemes promoted by the Colonial Development Corporation, which functions independently with its own loan capital, and seeks also, as does the British Government, to encourage private enterprise to invest capital in the Colonial field.

During the war, to counteract the shortage of fats, an Overseas Food Corporation was set up under the joint authority of the Ministry of Food and the Colonial Office, and amongst other enterprises this sponsored an ambitious scheme for groundnut cultivation in Tanganyika, but this venture was insufficiently explored in advance, and proved unsuccessful in operation, resulting in a heavy loss, although some good, if limited, results have been salvaged from the original scheme. The joint responsibility which did not work well in practice, was brought to an end, and the reorganized Corporation placed under the Colonial Office, and it now operates (through a local agricultural organization) in a restricted field in Tanganyika. Bad luck was also encountered by a poultry scheme in the Gambia, which had to be liquidated.

Generally speaking, however, a number of sound development schemes are going forward in many of the colonies which promise to add materially to the resources of those countries. It has been stressed moreover that this development policy involves no derogation from the rights and privileges or the responsibilities of the local legislatures, and the fact that a colony receives such assistance does not entail upon it any measure of financial control. There is assistance and guidance from London, but no "strings" attached and no dictation: the initiative comes mainly from the bodies themselves.

It may be noted here that the British colonies have been and are greatly indebted for valuable co-operation in the fields of medicine, education, social services and economic development on the part of American institutions such as the Rockefeller Foundation, the Carnegie Corporation and the Phelps-Stokes Fund, and to other bodies, individuals and government agencies. The thanks of the British Government had been expressed for this generous aid, and the United States Government is informed of British plans for colonial development.

The goal being thus declared and provision made for its eventual attainment, what are the difficulties to be overcome on the way? It is not possible to indicate here all the problems which await solution in the colonies. Apart from those of a general nature which affect all or most of the territories, individual colonies have their own particular problems, some of which have been noticed in the geographical survey. Some of the outstanding problems must however be briefly referred to here.

STANDARDS OF LIVING

The fundamental problem affecting many but by no means all of the colonial peoples is the comparatively low standard of living of the bulk of the population, and with that are bound up questions of nutrition and health, and of economic development. Standards of life are of course relative to the community under consideration, its habits, environment, and the stage of social and economic development which it has reached. It would obviously be absurd to apply the same standards to a primitive African tribe or to South Sea islanders who live in a tropical climate and whose wants are few and easily supplied, as to an industrialized community in Europe. Nonetheless it remains broadly true that the standards of living and nutrition are still too low in many of the colonies, despite the steady progress which has been made in recent years. Present conditions undoubtedly represent a great improvement upon those which existed, especially in Africa, before the advent of British rule, but much still remains to be done, particularly in view of the increasing impact of Western civilization upon these communities.

COLONIAL POLICY AND PROBLEMS

Not every colony has valuable mineral resources to be developed, and chief reliance must be placed upon the improvement of agriculture, dairying and livestock, both for consumption and for marketing, in order to provide revenues to raise the standard of living, nutrition and social services. In the majority of the colonies, agriculture must form the backbone of their economy, and it is therefore of primary importance to concentrate on improving methods of cultivation and of animal health and breeding, of training more agricultural officers and carrying out experimental research.

Apart from home consumption, an important element in the marketing of export crops is the effect of fluctuations in world prices for colonial products. This was especially felt in the West Indies when, after a period of relative prosperity, there was an acute fall in the world demand and price for sugar, which was also affected by the competition of sugar beet. Conditions have since improved, and there is an agreement with this country governing the quantities to be supplied and the price to be paid for West Indian sugar. In West Africa, marketing boards control the prices of cocoa and other commodities, and their accumulated reserves to act to some extent as a buffer on fluctuations. Other commodities affected by world fluctuations are obviously rubber in Malaya and tin in both Malaya and Nigeria.

In addition to these considerations, a very serious factor affecting the standard of living of colonial peoples is the constant pressure of population. Lord Boyd-Orr and the Food and Agriculture Organization of the United Nations have drawn attention to the constant tendency in the less developed countries for the population to increase and to encroach upon food supplies and upon any improvements secured in the standard of living. This is a problem in many colonies, in the West Indies for example, and in Africa and Malaya as well as the wider world, and it is one which is very difficult to deal with except over a long period and by raising educational and social standards. But it is obvious that even a comparatively small rise in the standard of living, say of the order of 5 to 10 per cent, spread over some 70,000,000 people would make a great difference, not only to the health and efficiency of the people themselves and to the development of their countries, but also to British and world trade, and there is no question that the colonies possess the natural resources and human capacity to effect that and a greater order of improvement.

NUTRITION

Just before the Second World War, a valuable report upon Nutrition in the Colonial Empire was issued by the Colonial Office, which has also set up an organization to carry out nutritional surveys in the various colonies. Despite the interruption of war, several of these studies have been completed and the work is still going on. The Committee, presided over by Earl De la Warr, came to the conclusion that the two main causes of malnutrition, apart from the prevalence of weakening diseases, were the low standard of living due to the poverty of the community (not necessarily in terms of money) and to ignorance, coupled in many cases with prejudice, in regard to methods of food preparation.

The report set forth many practical recommendations for tackling the problem, of which the most important were increased home production of foods for family consumption, including greater variety in diet, better methods of animal husbandry, and of storing and cooking foods, and especially wider provision for education in domestic science for women and children. Since the war, steady progress has been made, especially in Africa, and with the aid of development and welfare funds, both with the nutritional surveys and in carrying out the recommendations of the Report.

HEALTH

Reference to the prevalence of weakening diseases brings up the question of the general health of colonial peoples. Poverty, malnutrition, and disease are generally bound up together, but some diseases are endemic in the soil, especially in Africa, where the soil is often deficient in vital elements. Specific diseases will be presently alluded to, but apart from these, there is wide scope for effort in matters of elementary hygiene and in the provision of health and medical services.

Public health and personal hygiene are evidently the product of education, engineering and medical science, for it is a question not only of training people and especially children in elementary rules of health and feeding, and combating superstition and prejudice, but also of providing sanitation, pure water supplies, drainage and sewerage, and on the medical side, clinics, dispensaries, health visitors, nurses, hospitals and medical supplies and services generally.

It is only necessary to peruse some of the valuable annual reports issued by the Bureau of Hygiene and Tropical Diseases, summarizing medical and sanitary progress throughout the colonies, to see what is being done, often with exiguous resources and under most difficult conditions, and also the vast amount of leeway still to be made up. Here is an immense field for training men and women of the colonies, particularly in Africa, for nursing, health and medical work among their own people. It is being done already in West and East Africa, in the West Indies, in the South Seas and elsewhere, and many men and women are also being sent to complete their training in this country, but the present trickle needs to become a flood.

Coupled with health work, and as a necessary basis for action, is the need for further and fuller vital statistics in all the colonies. In the past, and especially with the interruption and shortages caused by two world wars, the colonies have lagged far behind other more advanced countries in this basic matter of vital statistics, and even the enumeration of the people at long intervals was far more often a process of guesswork than of computation; but past deficiencies, especially of skilled staffs and of educating the people in these matters, are now being gradually overcome, and a strong statistical department at the Colonial Office and corresponding officers in the colonies (though still inadequate in many places) are beginning to provide the vital data upon which alone informed and effective action can be taken.

Pests and Diseases

The British colonies, being mainly tropical or subtropical, naturally have their full share of pests and diseases, and the war against these must be waged unceasingly. With the success of that warfare is closely bound up the health and efficiency of the colonial peoples. Great strides have been made, especially in recent years, in combating the more serious pests and diseases, but a wide field for action remains. Some of the worst diseases of the past, such as the dreaded "yellow jack", have now been virtually conquered, and the conditions which earned for West Africa in the old days the unenviable name of the "white man's grave" no longer obtain in any serious degree. But the most widespread of tropical diseases, malaria, still takes a heavy toll not only in lives but in impaired health and efficiency, though the fight is on to reduce its ravages.

Here prevention is conspicuously better than cure, and a determined and systematic campaign can entirely eliminate the incidence of malaria from a whole country. This has been done for example in Cyprus and Mauritius and similar campaigns are being prosecuted elsewhere. Malaria is caused by a germ carried by the female of the *Anopheles* mosquito. This was the great discovery of Sir Ronald Ross, and he also discovered the means of attack by draining away stagnant waters and pools, or oiling their surface where drainage was not possible, thus preventing the mosquitoes breeding. This obviously requires constant vigilance and expenditure, and large-scale operations which cannot yet be undertaken everywhere. Meantime quinine dosage is extensively used as a remedy, and the cinchona, from the bark of which quinine is extracted, is being cultivated in several colonies, especially in East Africa.

Yaws is another debilitating disease from which many Africans suffer, the infection penetrating the skin through the soles of bare feet. Obviously any rise in economic standards which would bring about the wider use of footwear would prove an effective counter-measure. Blindness from infection of the eyes in childhood is another lamentable malady, and this is now being vigorously attacked by hygienic and other remedies. One of the greatest scourges in tropical countries, both in

Africa and the Pacific, has been leprosy, which has led to much devoted missionary and medical work, and there is now a strongly organized campaign throughout the colonies to combat this dread disease, which is beginning to show encouraging results. The advance of hygiene and medicine, and improved nutrition, will undoubtedly do most to put down such diseases in the future.

There still remain however the natural pests which are not so amenable to control, such as the tsetse fly and the locust. The sleeping sickness carried by the tsetse fly attacks both men and animals and has rendered large tracts of Africa practically uninhabitable, especially for livestock. A vigorous concerted campaign has been undertaken against this pest in several African territories, which has taken many forms, including systematic spraying from the air, and even the wholesale evacuation of inhabitants of infested areas with their livestock, until the bush country which the fly frequents is cleared and cleaned. Great headway has been made in Tanganyika, Nigeria and elsewhere, and the campaign is still proceeding, though, like the locust pest, it really requires international action. Rinderpest also attacks the native's cattle, often his chief form of wealth, and requires drastic veterinary counter measures not always easily enforced.

The swarms of locusts which periodically destroy great areas of crops in Africa and do enormous damage have by patient research, in which several countries have co-operated, been traced to their breeding grounds, and the only really effective action is to destroy them there before they start to migrate. An international locust organization has been set up, with the co-operation of the colonial powers and indigenous states in Africa, but the locust colonies often breed in remote and inaccessible spots and it is not always easy to take effective action before the swarm occurs.

Only some of the pests and diseases which afflict British colonial territories have been mentioned here and the fight against them is long and difficult, but of late years the resources of science, of trained personnel, and especially of the necessary funds, have been mobilized against them with increasing success, and as the people themselves learn to co-operate more actively in the campaign, a great and beneficient change will be visible over all this wide field in the years to come.

Soil Erosion

Soil erosion is largely a man-made problem. Many wide tracts of the earth which are now desert and sterile, as in Mesopotamia, the Sahara and the "dust-bowl" region of America, were once fertile, but their protective covering and trees having been steadily denuded by reckless exploitation or the effects of shifting cultivation, rainfall and floods have washed away the top soil and erosion has set in. The Tennessee Valley Authority is an object-lesson in what can be done on a large scale to cure even the worst dust-bowl, and on a smaller scale the patient labours of agricultural colonists in Israel have made the desert to blossom as the rose; but in Africa, the process is still continuing. The vast area of the Sahara, for example, is still extending, and drastic efforts must now be, and indeed are being, made to halt it and to reverse the cycle. Farther south, in the Kalahari too, schemes of irrigation and cultivation are being initiated, and in all the colonial territories where erosion threatens, the governments are alert to the danger.

There are many lines of attack. Shifting cultivation, for example, must be discouraged and new and improved methods of agriculture introduced. Roving herds of cattle must be controlled and reduced, and better methods of breeding livestock inculcated amongst native peoples. Where trees or bush have been extensively burned or cut down, afforestation must be started. Ridge draining and terracing must be undertaken where the top soil has been washed away by heavy rainfall, and in many areas dams must be built to control the flood waters.

These and other measures are now being actively carried out in many parts of Africa and in other colonies, but in Africa especially concerted effort on a large scale is required if effective results are to be secured, and this means intercolonial and indeed international action to support and supplement, not to supersede, all the individual effort that is being undertaken.

The field for forestry work in most of the colonies, and for irrigation and water-supply in some, is a very wide one, and means more trained staff and increased expenditure, but it is essentially reproductive work which in time will amply repay all the labour and money spent upon it. The same is even more true of agricultural methods and research, and improvements in veterinary science and animal health, to say nothing of improvements and extensions of fisheries in those colonies which are in part dependent on the harvest of sea and river. In all these fields active research and developments are taking place.

Education

Amongst colonial problems, we have left to the last perhaps the largest field of all. Education in the widest sense of the term is the key to most other colonial problems, social, economic and political. It is of fundamental importance in practically all the colonies, and indeed these basic questions of living, nutrition, health, and of agricultural, technical and domestic training, are all inextricably bound up together. Much has been done and is now being attempted in all spheres of education, but it has to be recorded that all this hopeful and interesting work, carried out both directly by colonial governments and native administrations, and especially by missionary and other voluntary agencies, represents but a small percentage of the vast field still to be covered. A comprehensive view of the problem will be found in the latest edition of Mr. Arthur Mayhew's *Education in the Colonial Empire*, mentioned in the Bibliography. Only a few outstanding points can be indicated in the space available here.

The humble but potent basis of all educational effort in the colonies, especially in Africa, is the "bush" school or its equivalent. It is an encouraging portent for the success of all such work that the African as a rule is eager for education and will go to any trouble and effort to obtain it, and although the motive force is generally a simple belief in the magic efficacy of this mysterious "education" as the source of the white man's power, the eagerness is welcome and helpful. Many native teachers are found who give themselves with wholehearted and selfless devotion to the work of teaching not only children but often also their elders in these bush schools, and the greatly increased supply of such teachers is of basic importance. It is a very good sign too that native administrations are generally keen to provide facilities and to pay for education out of their own treasuries. It now fully realized, as it was not at first, that the education of women and girls, especially in all matters concerned with domestic science, health and nutrition, is of the greatest importance, for in teaching the women you teach the whole family.

Powerful aids to popular and adult education have been enlisted in broadcasting and the cinema, and much valuable experimental and propagandist work has been already done in these fields throughout Africa, Malaya and elsewhere. Campaigns of mass literacy have been carried out with much success, and even amongst the still illiterate, the methods adopted to instruct the people in procedure at elections and in the issues raised are all contributing to the educational campaign. Broadcasting in particular has made great strides in the colonies. Most of the colonies have their own public broadcasting systems, staffed largely by personnel trained in this country, and wide coverage has been greatly aided by the development of a cheap receiver adapted to tropical conditions (originally known as the "saucepan" radio from its shape).

All colonial stations benefit greatly from the General Overseas programmes of the BBC, and also originate excellent programmes of their own. The good work that can be done in the early stages was exemplified by the rise of communal village radio in India, and this also played its part in the colonies. Radio raises of course the question of the numerous vernacular tongues (and all elementary teaching is best in the vernacular), but such difficulties are fully worth the trouble and cost of surmounting, and as the knowledge of English (particularly basic English) spreads, as it is bound to do, the radio and the sound picture will become tremendous vehicles for its further dissemination. The Colonial Film Unit is doing good work in the latter field, and the supply of good colonial films, especially documentary and demonstration films, is steadily increasing.

Colonial educational policy has a relatively short history. As a coherent whole, it may be said to take its rise from the appointment by the Secretary of State in 1923 of an Advisory Committee on Native Education in Tropical Africa, the scope of which was extended in 1929 to the colonies generally. This committee of experts working in London, with its joint secretaries (the late) Sir Hanns Vischer and Mr. Arthur Mayhew, has done and still does valuable co-ordinating and directive, work for education throughout the colonies, and it also publishes a useful quarterly review *Overseas Education*, which (with the annual colonial reports) records the progress made in the educational field. The Secretary of State now has an Educational Adviser, appointed on the same basis as the other expert advisers, but the labours of the Committee continue actively as before.

A great deal still remains to be done in the elementary field. At an earlier stage, it was estimated that out of some 5,000,000 children in British tropical Africa, only 30 per cent were receiving instruction of any kind, and although much has been done in recent years, the position cannot yet be considered satisfactory. Such education is still largely in the hands of missionary and other voluntary bodies; much of it is good, some of it is indifferent or poor. One thing is certain, that popular education is not a matter for education departments alone, but calls for the concerted effort of all departments concerned with the improvement of the people, health, education and so forth, and much of it must be given by way of practical demonstration rather than by formal instruction.

It might be considered that in view of the incompleteness of the foundations, the amount of attention that has been given to Higher Education throughout the colonies involves a danger of rearing a top-heavy structure, but there is some justification for this seeming anomaly. In the first place, there is the urgent need for the training of large numbers of indigenous teachers as a prerequisite for any considerable expansion of primary education; again we have special obligations to train the sons of chiefs for their duties in leadership, as well as of many more recruits for the local civil services and native administrations;

and finally there are the legitimate aspirations of increasing numbers of keen students in all the colonies for the full provision of educational facilities up to university standard.

In all the colonies this higher educational provision is being steadily improved and strengthened, and several recent commissions of inquiry, such as those on higher education in East and West Africa and in Malaya, have put forward far-reaching recommendations which are being implemented. The general intention is to provide facilities in all the larger colonial groups from the primary school up to the university. Colleges already exist in several colonies which are being developed into institutions of university rank, and others are being established.

Until recent years, much too little attention had been paid to technical education at all levels, but this serious deficiency is at last being tackled. In many colonies, especially in Africa, educational policy, partly because of its missionary origins, has been somewhat lopsided, and it must be confessed that the African himself has chiefly been eager for literacy, but the balance is now being redressed. As he proved during the war, the African, when properly trained, makes a good mechanic, and teaching in skilled crafts is now being increasingly provided. At a higher level, technical colleges are being set up, and with the training of more skilled instructors, a badly needed expansion in this department will be possible.

Amongst the institutions already well known are the famous Achimota College in the Gold Coast, founded by Sir Gordon Guggisberg and owing much to the example of Dr. Aggrey, which occupies a unique position in African education, and caters for every branch of training; University College at Ibadan, Nigeria; Fourah Bay College in Sierra Leone; Makerere College in Uganda, which has a great future before it; the Jeanes School in Kenya, which owes much to the aid of the Phelps-Stokes fund; and the Tabora School in Tanganyika. The work done at Fort Hare in South Africa is outside the colonial field but has much influence on African education, and there is now the new inter-racial university founded at Salisbury, Southern Rhodesia, for the Central African Federation. Thus there will be universities for West, East and Central Africa, and for the West Indies, which already has the old established Codrington

College in Barbados and the new university college in Jamaica.

In other colonies too similar provision exists or will be available; Raffles College and the Medical School in Singapore form the nucleus of a University for Malaya, and it is significant that it is also proposed to found a Chinese university for Malaya. As already noted, the University of Hong Kong has done splendid work not only for the colony but also for Chinese students from the mainland. Malta, as we have seen, has its own university, founded over two centuries ago, but it is a pity that there is not yet a similar institution in Cyprus.

With all this varied educational work proceeding in the different colonies, which presumably have much to learn from each other, it would seem there is scope for a general conference on Colonial Education in London, just as there is for similar conferences on colonial agriculture, engineering, and public works, health and hygiene and other main divisions of colonial work; some of these indeed are held from time to time.

Students Welfare and Colour

In connexion with higher education in the colonies, reference must be made to the question of colonial students in this country. At present there are between 5,000 and 6,000 men and women from the colonies, of all races, studying in this country, and although, as facilities for higher studies develop in the colonies, their numbers may be expected eventually to diminish (although there will always be interchange of teachers and at least post-graduate work done here) their presence amongst us offers certain problems.

Their personal interests and studies are looked after by the Welfare Department of the Colonial Office from the moment of their arrival in this country. The great majority come here under the auspices of their own governments, and the Welfare Department is in touch with the educational authorities in the various colonies, but some are sent directly by their parents or have their own resources, but these are equally entitled, if they wish, to the services of the Welfare Department or of the Crown Agents. Where they are not actually resident at the

University or other institution to which they are attached (and this is by far the best solution) the department prefers that they should live if possible with private families, so that they should acquire first-hand knowledge of English ways of life, and it maintains registers of approved lodgings for this purpose; but often on arrival or even later, such arrangements are not possible, and accordingly in London and other large centres special hostels have been provided for the accommodation of colonial students.

At first these hostels were under the direct administration of the Colonial Office, but as this might have implied in the minds of students some kind of official supervision, it was thought better to transfer this work to the British Council, which is not an official body, and by them excellent arrangements are made for the personal and social needs of the students. Outstanding examples of such centres in London are London House, Bloomsbury, administered by a separate trust and mainly for post-graduate students from the senior nations of the Commonwealth but accepting colonial students equally, and the Hans Place hostel, but there are other hostels both in London and the provinces which are doing valuable work in providing congenial backgrounds for the lives and studies of colonial students while in this country. They also have their own bodies, such as the West African Students Union, the Malayan Union and others.

Both the British Council and the various empire societies and other voluntary bodies arrange social contacts, vacation visits and travel and other opportunities for the students of getting to know the country whilst here, and the majority diligently pursue their studies and enjoy their stay, but some undoubtedly have unfortunate experiences, either in unsuitable lodgings or in other surroundings or influences that may send them back to their countries embittered or at least unfavourably impressed by their stay here. This is the more to be regretted since many of these young men may well become leaders in their own country. Especially unfortunate is it if they become the victims of colour prejudice here when there is no trace of it in their country of origin.

Unhappily colour prejudice is a very difficult and complex

human problem for which there is no easy solution, but it is a problem of obviously vital importance to this world-wide multi-racial Commonwealth, which is numerically at least overwhelmingly a coloured Commonwealth. That people of different races can live happily and in complete equality together is shown by various examples such as that of Maori and Pakeha (white man) in New Zealand, but the problem is much more difficult in some of our plural communities. It must be remembered also that colour prejudice operates both ways, as Sir Alan Burns points out in his wise and thoughtful book on this subject, and sometimes it has mainly an economic basis, as in the case of white and coloured workers in mines and other industries. We have however a special responsibility to avoid its expression in the heart of the Commonwealth, and to treat all our colonial fellow-citizens as guests and friends in our midst.

There are also the coloured workers who, being British subjects, are free to come here from various colonies, and often do so regardless of the prospects of their employment. These raise problems of another kind, industrial and social.

When the colonial universities and other higher educational institutions are fully developed, the situation will of course be different, and for the most part only the senior and more experienced students will come here and to other centres in the Commonwealth for post-graduate work or simply for personal experience in travel, but it is highly desirable that there should always be constant interchange between the peoples, and especially the younger people, of all the countries of the Commonwealth, and this should take place under the happiest auspices.

It has been alleged against us in the past that we have failed to win the goodwill of many of the intelligentzia in the colonies, and that these have often become disgruntled and antagonistic to the administration. Many have taken up their studies in the expectation of securing government posts on completing them, and have been disappointed and turned their energies into political channels. In this new era of development and transition to self-government, there should be far wider opportunities of utilizing all the available talent in the various countries, and of regulating the flow in some closer approximation to anticipated needs, for there can be no doubt that all these countries will increasingly require the services of their own educated men and women not only in the civil service but also in local government, in native administrations, in the professions and business, and in many other capacities in an expanding economy. Unfortunately at present too many students tend to take to the law rather than to medicine, engineering, agricultural science and other technical occupations which badly need recruits, but no doubt this will correct itself in time.

LOCAL GOVERNMENT, TRADE UNIONS AND CO-OPERATION

Finally, and as a kind of addendum to educational problems, we should glance briefly at the developments which are taking place in many of the colonies in the formation, reform or strengthening of local government bodies, service in which undoubtedly forms the best preparation for self-government in wider affairs, and at the active encouragement of trade unions and of co-operative movements which has been a feature of recent colonial policy. Colonial Governments are paying special attention to municipal and other local organizations both for their own sake as important elements in the general administrative structure, to accustom the people to the management of their own affairs, and to be able in time to draw upon a wider personnel for recruitment to the central government. In this and other Commonwealth countries, these bodies have long played an important and indeed essential part in the education and training of democracy and they should be enabled to fulfil a similar function in the colonies.

The Secretary of State has a Labour Adviser amongst his other experts, and in pursuance of our policy of encouraging workers' organizations, we have sent out officers of experience of British trade unions to advise as to trade-union organization in various colonies. Much good work has been done in this field, but it is not a natural growth among some colonial peoples as it is here, and more experience still needs to be gained, which is not surprising considering the long and difficult history of the trade-union movement even in this country. In the co-operative field, especially in various forms of agriculture and in producer co-operatives generally, as well as the consumer side, much more solid progress has been made in many colonies, and the movement shows many encouraging signs for the future.

We have only been able in this chapter to touch upon a few of the more outstanding among the many problems which beset the colonial scene. Any intelligent reader of the newspaper press will find others cropping up from time to time, and these should be studied against the background of the particular country and people, and in relation to our colonial policy as a whole. In a concluding chapter, some further general considerations will be referred to before attempting, however imperfectly, to sum up future trends in that living and growing organism which constitutes the emergent or colonial portion of the Commonwealth of nations.

CHAPTER XI

FUTURE TRENDS

THE free and voluntary association of equal partners in the original Commonwealth was made easier by the fact that these communities were of similar racial and cultural origin, with similar traditions, sentiments, political and social institutions all deriving from the mother country. The ties though intangible were rendered stronger and more durable by their underlying identity of origin and character. The balance was completely altered by the accession of India, Pakistan and Ceylon. Although these countries had been formed into a similar mould under British influence and readily adopted parliamentary institutions on the British model, background and tradition were necessarily quite different. The same applies to by far the largest portion of the emergent Commonwealth constituted by what has hitherto been known as the British colonial empire.

Political enfranchisement in these cases involves differences of kind rather than degree, and introduces many complications hitherto not apparent or important. Lord Hailey has dealt with this topic very suggestively in his Romanes lecture on the Place of the Colonies in the British Commonwealth. To state these difficulties is certainly not to imply that they cannot be solved, but only to recognize that their handling will require time, patience and practical statesmanship.

Although our declared objective is eventual self-government for all our colonies, this may take different forms according to the nature and circumstances of the particular community or country. In some cases there is no natural cohesion or homogeneity in a given colonial area, and this may seem to require adjustment of boundaries which would involve negotiation with other powers, as in some parts of Africa. Then either for this or for economic reasons, federation into a larger unit may become desirable or necessary. There is the question of what is the best form of self-government for peoples unfamiliar with

Western traditions but possessing indigenous institutions hitherto suited to their natural genius, but probably unfitted for modern conditions to which they have to be adapted? The question will probably prove academic in many cases, for most African, Asian and other peoples seem intent on securing for themselves the institutions which they believe hold the secret of success of the more advanced communities of the West, and these are regarded as legitimate political objectives and tests of our sincerity by most of our colonial peoples.

Apart from this, however, there is the more serious question of the future of plural or multi-racial communities in the present colonial system. It has yet to be discovered what is the permanent role of Europeans in countries which are primarily the natural habitat of the coloured races, but which have also become areas of European settlement. That for some time to come, especially in large parts of Africa, white men have a great part to play in leadership and guidance to the native races is indisputable, and co-operation or partnership on this basis should be of mutual benefit, but when with that aid the indigenous peoples have attained full political maturity, a different situation will have arisen. But it must be remembered that as trustees our responsibility extends to all the elements in such plural communities, and that it is our duty to ensure if possible that the legitimate interests of each are adequately safeguarded. The solution must lie in some form of equal partnership between the several races or elements in such communities, and not in the dominance of any one of them over the others. This applies not only in Africa but in such countries as Malaya, where the European element is inconsiderable and the population is divided between Malay, Chinese and Indian races. The best hope for all plural communities is to develop a new nationality based on equal citizenship of a common country.

Certainly there can be no future for *apartheid* or segregation, or any policy based on fear or suspicion, which seeks to impose permanent dominance by one race over others, and for that reason present trends in South Africa must be watched with considerable anxiety, not only in the true interests of South Africa itself but also because of their serious repercussions throughout British Africa.

Great Britain does not at present share her heavy colonial responsibilities with any other member nation of the Commonwealth, although doubtless colonial questions are from time to time discussed at Commonwealth conferences, but as the senior circle is enlarged by the accession of further units into the ranks of self-governing territories, it becomes a question whether this does not impose at least some moral obligation upon the Commonwealth as a whole. It is probable that Great Britain would not wish to share her responsibility until her trusteeship is completely and honourably discharged, but it would seem desirable that the welfare of the present "junior partners" should concern the whole Commonwealth. That there is readiness to accept wider responsibility is shown by the initiation of the Colombo Plan, which covers South and South-East Asia. Both the present senior partners and those units emerging into self-government should be interested in the further progress of the remaining colonies.

This is primarily a question of education. It must be admitted that at present the peoples of the various countries of the Commonwealth are not very well informed about their fellow members. We in this country do know something, though by no means enough, about the other senior members, but even now the British public are none too well informed about the colonies for which they are responsible, and it is certain that the peoples of the other "dominions" know less, and that the colonies themselves are little interested in each other. If the peoples of the Commonwealth are to strengthen their links with each other or even to remain a coherent whole, this regrettable deficiency in mutual knowledge certainly calls for remedy. So far at least as we in Great Britain are concerned, this education should begin in the schools, where both the teaching and the text-books should emphasize from the outset that every child is a potential citizen not only of this country but of a world-wide Commonwealth of nations. It is not enough that some perfunctory attention should be given to this as an additional "subject" on the fringe of a crowded syllabus, but it should permeate and form an integral part of the history and geography taught and of the curriculum as a whole. The world has completely changed since Britain was herself a self-sufficient world power, and we survive and exercise our proper influence today only as a member of the Commonwealth. If we were to take the lead in this matter, our example might be followed by other members of the Commonwealth.

The foregoing is perhaps a digression from our proper theme, though a very serious matter in itself. To return to the future of the colonies, it may be argued that as the colonial relationship which has subsisted in world history for so long a period is now recognized to be passing away, the welfare of peoples still in a state of tutelage is a collective responsibility of civilization, and this principle is in fact accepted by the United Nations and the so-called "colonial charter" is largely based on British colonial policy. But international recognition of colonial responsibility certainly does not imply international *administration* of colonies. This would not prove workable in practice, nor would it be in the interests of the colonial peoples themselves, which of course must be the governing consideration.

In all cases colonial peoples have become accustomed to the methods and traditions, the laws, customs and even language of their rulers, their thoughts and aspirations have been formed in a particular mould, and even where their own culture and civilization persist, to attempt to replace the institutions and administration with which they are familiar by an impersonal body of international personnel owning no common tradition, and even possibly with conflicting ideals and methods, would be something totally beyond the grasp of most colonial peoples, who need personal guidance and an example upon which they can model their own action.

Moreover, it must be remembered that the process of fitting colonial peoples for self-government necessarily implies the progressive and increasing association of the people themselves in the task of administration at all stages until eventually they take over completely. This process would be rendered far more difficult by the relative inelasticity, complexity and remoteness of an international administration. But these objections do not apply to a Commonwealth or Overseas service, such as is now proposed, which would take over the traditions of the present Colonial Service. Granted this framework, however, there is scope for the co-operation of other nationals even beyond the Commonwealth, and especially of technicians and specialists of all kinds, provided the prior claims of the indigenous peoples be always borne in mind. In this way colonial administration might become increasingly cosmopolitan to the benefit of both rulers and of ruled, without breaking the national mould or spirit or impairing the responsibility of individual colonial powers.

Whilst the objective of our colonial policy is declared to be self-government within the Commonwealth, it must of course be recognized that as soon as a colony has taken over responsibility for its own affairs, it is free by reason of that very fact to elect for independence either within or (as Burma did) outside the Commonwealth. Just as the present members of the Commonwealth have the right to secede if they wish (a right which the Irish republic exercised) so it is fully understood that there can be no suggestion of compulsion in the voluntary association of free and equal peoples. Each must form its own judgement of where its true and ultimate interest lies.

The economic relations of the colonies are also of great importance, and colonial trade, both with Britain and the rest of the Commonwealth, and with the world generally, is bound to become an increasingly prominent factor in the future. Some measure of its importance is indicated by the fact that the total trade of the colonies in 1953 was of the order of about £1,400,000,000 each of imports and of exports and this will certainly increase steadily as development proceeds. The colonies are already participating in Commonwealth economic conferences, being represented not only by the Secretary of State but in some cases by their own ministers.

The policy of imperial preference may undergo some modification if there is a tendency towards freer trade in the world generally, but already over great areas, especially in Africa, by international agreement apart from mandatory obligation, free trade exists for all on equal terms, and even where some preference is given to British goods, this seldom has the effect of excluding those of other nations. For example, Japanese textiles sell freely in East Africa.

Responsible colonial statesmen like the late Lord Lugard

advocated a return to our earlier practice of equal economic opportunity for all throughout the colonies, and this would certainly be in accordance with the principle of the "dual mandate". On the long view, and in a world economic order freed from artificial barriers and restrictions (which is not in sight yet) it might also be best for the colonial peoples themselves, but we have to remember that we stand in a fiduciary relation to them, and under present conditions they may wish to retain some bargaining power in their own hands when they take over full responsibility for their own trade.

Nor can we consider the British colonies solely in relation to the Commonwealth. They will have their own place in the world to fill, and there is the question of their relations with neighbouring peoples, particularly in Africa and in south-east Asia. As we have seen, Africa was somewhat arbitrarily parcelled out amongst various European powers, with the result today that developments in any one part of the continent inevitably have wider repercussions. Co-operation between the various colonial powers in Africa is already well established, but this may have eventually to be broadened even to include political adjustments.

There should be a co-ordinated scheme of development at least for Africa south of the Sahara based on Lord Hailey's survey or some wider plan, backed by international agreement and guarantee, including the provision of the necessary funds. There may have to be in some form a Council of Africa, representative not only of the powers directly concerned, but also of others such as the United States, and upon which the emergent African peoples in turn shall find their rightful place. Such a Council might be either separate from or form a regional subsidiary body to the United Nations.

At the heart of the colonial system, the central machinery of colonial government will have to be continuously and progressively adapted to keep pace with political and economic developments in the colonies themselves. The Colonial Office has already been considerably transformed from what it was even two or three decades ago, and it must change even more in the future. By the time its new building in Westminster is completed, there may emerge a coalescence of the present two separate departments into a greater Commonwealth Office, for the existing purely "colonial" functions of the Colonial Office are bound to dwindle progressively in the future.

The transitional period may however be lengthy, and as it is of crucial significance both to the colonial peoples and to ourselves, it is essential that our trust should be informed with knowledge as well as with judgement. Parliament should maintain a close supervision over colonial affairs, and for this purpose it would probably be desirable that, apart from specially interested groups in the respective parties, a Parliamentary Joint Committee of both Houses could be set up to review the colonial scene and to consider proposed legislation in advance, as far as possible free from party bias.

So onerous is the burden now placed upon the shoulders of the Secretary of State and his assistant ministers and staff that it may be worth considering whether it would be desirable to set up a Colonial Council, including upon it some of our colonial elder statesmen and representatives from some of the colonies, to co-ordinate the activities of the various advisory committees and experts, and to formulate colonial policy "above the battle", as it were, of immediate events and interests.

Within the limits of this small volume, it has obviously been impossible to do more than introduce the reader to such a vast and complex subject as the British colonial empire, or as we prefer to call it, the emergent Commonwealth, concerned as it is with the lives and future of some 75,000,000 people of all races in some thirty-five countries, large and small, scattered across the globe, and forming part of a larger Commonwealth comprising a quarter of the world's inhabitants. To deal with such a subject adequately would require not one volume but many, and indeed other volumes in this series will be found to deal with some of the individual countries or groups; but it was rightly decided that the subject also required treatment, however superficially, as a whole.

The origin, growth and future evolution of the British colonial system is a fascinating study, one moreover which concerns all of us who are ultimately responsible for these peoples, and with a view to enable the reader or student to follow up this introduction, a select Bibliography, which it is hoped will indicate the principal sources of further information, has been completed. Here one may learn something of what life in these diverse countries is like, of its difficulties and drawbacks and equally of its compensations, of human imperfections and human greatness, of how Britain's colonial task is being accomplished without concealment or mitigation of faults, yet not without evidence of good qualities—a record of which on the whole, despite blemishes, we may be justly proud.

Much of this literature is critical and no small part of the criticism (and by no means the least trenchant) comes not from foreign or indigenous sources but from British writers some of whom have had personal experience and responsibility and some not, but all of whom enjoy the truly British privilege of self-criticism or self-depreciation. Then there are the straightforward accounts of things seen or done by travellers, settlers, explorers or officials, which bring the country or the people vividly to life; or the mature reflections of those who have borne heavy responsibility in the colonies, which may give us some understanding of the nature of the task. Especially should the reader not omit the lives of those men and women who in diverse ways have helped to build up or to administer this wide colonial heritage, for it is not so much the product of an impersonal system or policy as of human effort and personality.

In these days opportunities are increasing for visiting some of these countries, and there is nothing better than first-hand impressions to correct or supplement abstract theories or information, but as this still cannot be the good fortune of most of us, it may be useful to suggest that reading should where possible be reinforced by, for example, visits to the exhibition-galleries, cinema and lecture-rooms of the Imperial Institute in London. This institution dating from Victorian times it is now recommended should become the Commonwealth Institute, and as such a centre for Commonwealth activities and gatherings in London.

Our colonial task can only be successfully accomplished if the British and colonial peoples can work together in friendly co-operation for the agreed end of self-government. There are still many difficulties and dangers ahead, but the necessary basis of goodwill and mutual respect does exist, and despite many mistakes and shortcomings, the colonial peoples on the whole have been content to accept our rule and their status as British subjects, and until they can take over the management of their own affairs, have shown no desire to change their allegiance. It will be the greatest tribute to our essential integrity and fairness if we find in the years to come our former colonies standing, like India, Pakistan, and Ceylon, by our side as equal and free nations in a greater Commonwealth. "Colonialism" is destined to pass and the end of a dependent empire is already in sight: we have willed it so and willed both the end and the means.

The Commonwealth of the future and the United States, with their immense joint resources, not only in material power but by their faith in freedom and the principles of democracy, can if they stand together assure the safety and peace of the world.

BIBLIOGRAPHY

ALTHOUGH far from exhaustive, since that would necessitate a volume in itself, it is hoped that this guide to further reading will meet the needs not only of the ordinary reader but even of the serious student of colonial affairs. With a few exceptions, purely technical or specialized works are not included, and those who may wish to prosecute research in such fields are referred to the Libraries of the Colonial Office and the Royal Empire Society, where every assistance is gladly rendered to the serious inquirer. Detailed bibliographies of some of the colonies can also be consulted there.

Current information on the colonies is obtainable from the Colonial Office Information Department, from the Central Office of Information, from the Crown Agents for Overseas and from information offices maintained by individual colonies or groups of colonies in London. Particulars and addresses of these and other sources of information are given in a pamphlet entitled *The Colonies: a Guide to material and information Services available to the Schools and the Public*, issued by the first two departments named. Other bodies which from time to time issue papers on colonial subjects are the Royal Institute of International Affairs, the British Society for International Understanding, and the Imperial Institute. A valuable repository is the Institute of Commonwealth Studies of the University of London, and for African questions, the African Bureau.

The Cambridge History of The British Empire and its bibliographies is a basic source of general reference, but works on the Empire or Commonwealth as a whole are not included here. They are the subject of other volumes in this series, particulars of which can be found on page 187 of this book. They include Sir Ivor Jennings on *The British Commonwealth of Nations* and separate volumes on the "senior partners" in the Commonwealth and some of the colonies.

This Bibliography will first list outstanding publications and general works on the colonies and will then indicate selected books on individual colonies or groups, following the geographical order adopted in this book. As colonial affairs are of topical importance, new books are constantly appearing, and the reader may wish to note their titles on the end papers of this volume.

A valuable source of day to day information on colonial matters is the special periodical press such as *New Commonwealth*, *Corona*, *Today*, *The Times Review of British Colonies* (quarterly), and papers like *African World*, *East Africa and Rhodesia*, *West Africa*, *West African Review*, *West India Committee Circular*, *Great Britain and the East*, and *British Malaya*. In addition, each colony has of course its own local press, many examples of which can be seen in the Royal Empire Society's Library. There are also special journals such as *Oversea Education*, the *Journal of African Administration*, the *Commonwealth Survey*, and the journals of the various institutions referred to in this book.

Official Publications

All British official publications can be obtained from H.M. Stationery Office and Colonial Government publications from the Crown Agents, Millbank, London, S.W.1.

"The Colonial Office List", annual.

"Annual Reports on the individual Colonies"

"The Secretary of State's Annual Report to Parliament"

"Regional Reports on British Dependencies"

"Economic Survey of the Colonial Territories"

"Customs Tariffs of the Colonial Empire"

"The Digest of Colonial Statistics"

"Conditions and Cost of Living in the Colonial Empire"

"Regulations for H.M. Colonial Service, and Recruitment" (pamphlets)

"The Colonial Service as a Career," by Kenneth Bradley.

A series of official booklets introducing groups of colonies, and the volumes of the Corona Library.

In addition, White Papers or Blue-books are published from time to time dealing with colonial questions or special inquiries.

BIBLIOGRAPHY

GENERAL WORKS

Bertram, Sir A., *The Colonial Service*, 1930
Wyndham, H. A., *Problems of Trusteeship; Native Education*, 1933
Greaves, I. C., *Modern Production among Backward Peoples*, 1935
Clark, G., *Facts and Figures on Colonies*, 1936
Clark, G., *A Place in the Sun*, 1936
St. Johnston, Sir R., *Life in the Colonial Service*, 1936
International Colonial Institute, *Organisation Politique et Administrative des Colonies*, 1937
Macaulay, N., *Mandates; Reasons, Results, Remedies*, 1937
Kucynski, D., *Colonial Population*, 1937
Jeffries, Sir Chas., *The Colonial Empire and its Civil Service*, 1938
Fletcher, B. A., *Education and Colonial Development*, 1938
Mayhew, A., *Education in the Colonial Empire*, 1938
Clark, C., *The Crown Colonies and their History*, 1939
Papi, G. U., *The Colonial Problem*, 1939
Viljoen, S., *Economics of Primitive Peoples*, 1939
Murray, A. V., *The School in the Bush*, 1939
Jacks, G. V., and Whyte, R. O., *Rape of the Earth; Soil Erosion*, 1939
Scott, H. H., *History of Tropical Medicine*, 2 vols., 1939
Nutrition in the Colonial Empire, 2 parts (C.O.), 1939
Meresco, E., *Colonial Questions and Peace*, 1940
Troup, R. S., *Colonial Forest Administration*, 1940
Lugard, Lord, *The Dual Mandate*, 1941
Hailey, Lord, *Place of the Colonies in the Commonwealth*, 1941
Wright, M., *Development of the Legislative Council*, 1946
Parkinson, Sir Cosmo, *The Colonial Office from Within*, 1947
Cannington, C. E., *The British Overseas*, 1948
Jeffries, Sir Chas., *Partners for Progress*, 1949
Mair, L. P., *Welfare in the British Colonies*, 1949
Burns, Sir A., *Colour Prejudice*, 1950
Hall, H. D., *Mandates, Dependencies and Trusteeships*, 1950
Church, R. J. H., *Modern Colonization*, 1951
Jeffries, Sir C., *The Colonial Police*, 1952

THE WEST INDIES

St. Johnston, Sir R., *A West Indian Pepper-pot*, 1928
Newton, A. P., *European Nations in the West Indies*, 1933
Aspinall, Sir A., *Wayfarer in the West Indies*, 1934
Aspinall, Sir A., *Pocket Guide to the West Indies* (latest edition)
Rutter, Owen, *If Crab no Walk*, 1934

Macmillan, W. M., *Warning from the West Indies*, 1936
Burn, W. L., *Emancipation and Apprenticeship in the B.W.I.*, 1938
Makin, W. J., *Caribbean Nights*, 1939
Burn, W. L., *The British West Indies*, 1951
Luke, Sir H., *Caribbean Circuit*, 1953
Fermor, W. L., *Traveller's Tree*, 1953

BAHAMAS

Defries, A. D., *The Fortunate Isles*, 1929
Bell, H. M., *Bahamas, Isles of June*, 1934

BARBADOS

Harlow, V., *History of Barbados*, 1926
Savage, R., *Barbados, B.W.I.* 1937

LEEWARDS

Watkins, F. H., *Handbook of the Leeward Islands*

VIRGIN ISLANDS

Levo, J., *Virgin Islanders*, 1929

JAMAICA

Gaunt, M., *Reflections in Jamaica*, 1932
Olivier, Lord, *The Myth of Governor Eyre*, 1934
Olivier, Lord, *Jamaica, The Blessed Island*, 1936
Cundall, F., *Lady Nugent's Journal; Jamaica 130 Years Ago*, 1936
Cundall, F., *Governors of Jamaica in the 17th and 18th Centuries*, 1936–7
Mathieson, W. L., *Governor Eyre and the Sugar Colonies*, 1936
Olley, P. P., *Guide to Jamaica*, 1937

TRINIDAD

Reis, C., *History of the Constitution and Government of Trinidad*, 1929
Calder-Marshall, A., *Glory Dead*, 1939
Trinidad and Tobago Yearbook and Handbook

BRITISH HONDURAS

Burdon, Sir J., *Archives of British Honduras* (3 vols.), 1934–7

BRITISH GUIANA

Clementi, Lady, *Through British Guiana*, 1920
Webber, A. R. F., *Centenary History and Handbook of British Guiana*, 1931
Clementi, Sir C., *Constitutional History of British Guiana*, 1937
Ahmed, R., *I Rise; Story of a Negro* (B.G.), 1938
Mittelholzer, E., *Corentyne Thunder*, 1941

BERMUDA

Hayward, W. B., *Bermuda Past and Present*, 1923
Strode, H., *The Story of Bermuda*, 1932
Wilkinson, H., *The Adventurers of Bermuda*, 1933
Kerr, W. B., *Bermuda and the American Revolution*, 1937

ATLANTIC

Boyson, V. F., *Falkland Islands*, 1924
Goebel, J., *The Struggle for the Falkland Islands*, 1927
Matthews, L. H., *South Georgia*, 1931
Ommanney, D., *South Latitude*, 1938
Rymill, J. A., and Mill, H. R., *Southern Lights*, 1939
Gane, D. M., *Tristan da Cunha*, 1932
Christopherson, E., *Tristan, the Lonely Isle*, 1940
Crawford, A. H., *I Went to Tristan*, 1941

AFRICA GENERALLY

Smith, Rev. E. W., *The Golden Stool*, 1926
Buell, R. L., *Problem of the African Peoples* (2 vols.), 1928
Evans, Ivor L., *The British in Tropical Africa*, 1929
Lugard, Lord, *The Dual Mandate in British Tropical Africa*, 1932
Duff, Sir H., *African Small Chop*, 1932
Trevor, T. G., *Forty Years in Africa*, 1932
Bradley, K., *Africa Notwithstanding*, 1932
Strickland, C. F., *Co-operation for Africa*, 1933
Davis, J. Merle, *Modern Industry and the African*, 1933
Orde-Browne, J., *The African Labourer*, 1933

Worthington, S. and E. B., *Inland Waters of Africa*, 1934
Werner, Dr. A., *Bantu Legends*, 1934
Reynolds, A. J., *African Passage*, 1935
Gorer, G., *African Dances*, 1935
Mair, Dr. L. P., *Native Policies in Africa*, 1936
Ludwig, E., *The Nile from the Source to Egypt*, 1937
Young, T. Cullen, *African Ways and Wisdom*, 1937
Balfour, P., *Lords of the Equator*, 1937
Tilman, H. W., *Snow on the Equator*, 1937
Trowell, M., *African Arts and Crafts*, 1938
Hailey, Lord, *An African Survey*, and supplementary vols., 1938
Macmillan, W. M., *Africa Emergent*, 1938
Leith-Ross, Mrs., *African Women*, 1939
Juned, H. P., *Bantu Heritage*, 1939
Westermann, D., *The African Today and Tomorrow*, 1939
Perham, M., *Britain in Africa*, 1940; *Ten Africans*, 1940; *Africans and British Rule*, 1941
Forbes, M., and Evans, Pritchard, *African Political Systems* (British Rule, 1941)
Pim, Sir A., *Financial and Economic History of the African Territories*, 1941
Cary, Joyce, *The Case for African Freedom*, 1941
Hailey, Lord, *Native Administration and Political Development in British Africa*
Farson, N., *Behind God's Back*, 1941; *Last Chance in Africa*, 1951
Crocker, W. R., *On Governing Colonies (Africa)*, 1947
Bartlett, Vernon, *Struggle for Africa*, 1953
Stamp, L. D., *Africa Strides in Tropical Development*, 1953
Keppel-Jones, Arthur, *South Africa*, 1953

WEST AFRICA

Kingsley, Mary, *West African Studies*, 1899
Martin, E. C., *The British West African Settlements*, 1927
Butt-Thompson, F. W., *West African Secret Societies*, 1929
Schweitzer, Dr. A., *The Primeval Forest*, 1931
Jones, G. Howard, *The Earth Goddess*, 1937
Stebbing, Prof. E. P., *The Forests of West Africa and the Sahara*, 1937
Blake, J. W., *European Beginnings in West Africa*, 1938
Meek, C. K., Macmillan and Hussey, *Lectures on European Impact on West Africa*, 1940
Huxley, Elspeth, *The Four Guineas*, 1954

Reeve, H. F., *The Gambia; its History ancient and modern*, 1912
Hardinge, R., *Gambia and Beyond*, 1934
Gray, J. M., *A History of the Gambia*, 1940
Southorn, Lady, *The Gambia*, 1950
Butt-Thompson, F. W., *Sierra Leone in History and Tradition*, 1926
Migeod, F. W. H., *A View of Sierra Leone*, 1926
Gervis, P., *Sierra Leone Story*, 1951
Lewis, Roy, *Sierra Leone*
Cardinall, A. W., *The Gold Coast*, 1931, and other works
Rattray, R. S., *Ashanti*, 1923-4
Claridge, W. W., *History of the Gold coast and Ashanti* (2 vols.), 1925
Redmayne, P., *The Gold Coast Yesterday and Today*, 1938
Ward, N. E. F., *History of the Gold Coast*, 1951
Meek, C. K., *Northern Tribes of Nigeria* (2 vols.), 1925
Talbot, P. A., *Peoples of Southern Nigeria* (4 vols), 1926
Geary, Sir W. M., *Nigeria Under British Rule*, 1927
Hogben, S. J., *Mohammedon Emirates of Nigeria*, 1930
Hastings, A. C., *Nigerian Days*, 1931
Haig, E. F. G., *Nigerian Sketches*, 1932
Hives, F., *Ju-Ju and Justice in Nigeria*, 1932
Burns, Sir Alan, *History of Nigeria*, 1942
Crocker, W. R., *Nigeria and British Colonial Administration*, 1936
Meek, C. K., *Law and Authority in a Nigerian Tribe*, 1937
Perham, M., *Native Administration in Nigeria*, 1937
Miller, W., *Yesterday and Tomorrow in N. Nigeria*, 1939
Basden, G. T., *Niger Ibos*, 1939
Ferry, F., *Mad Dogs and Englishmen*, 1941
Forde, D., and Scott, R., *Economics of Nigeria* (2 vols.), 1947
Rudin, H. R., *Germans in the Cameroons*, 1938
Kuczynski, R. R., *The Cameroons and Togoland*, 1939

EAST AND CENTRAL AFRICA

Roscoe, J., *25 Years in East Africa*, 1921
Church, A. J., *East Africa, a new Dominion*, 1927
Joelson, F. S., *East Africa Today and Tomorrow*, 1934
Thurnwald, R. C., *Black and White in East Africa*, 1936
Swynnerton, Dr. C. F., *The Tsetse Flies of East Africa*, 1937
Coupland, Sir R., *East Africa and its Invaders*, 1938; *Exploitation of E. Africa*, 1939
Huxley, Elspeth, *East Africa*, 1941
Orde-Browne, G. J., *The Vanishing Tribes of Kenya*, 1925

Hobley, C. W., *Kenya from Chartered Company to Crown Colony*, 1929

Weller, H. O., *Kenya without Prejudice*, 1931

Mockerie, P. G., *An African speaks for his People*, 1934

Huxley, Elspeth, *White Mans' Country (Lord Delamere)* (2 vols.), 1935

Leakey, L. S. B., *Stone Age Cultures and Races of Kenya*, 1935

Leakey, L. S. B., *Kenya Contrasts and Problems*, 1936; *White African*, 1937

Watteville, V. de, *Speak to the Earth*, 1935

Dilley, Dr. M. R., *British Policy in Kenya*, 1938

Kenyatta, J., *Facing Mount Kenya; Tribal Life of the Kikuyu*, 1938

Cranworth, Lord, *Kenya Chronicles*, 1939

Peristiany, J. G., *Social Institutions of the Kipsigis*, 1940

Jones, H. G., *Uganda in Transformation*, 1926

Day, A. J., *Sunshine and Rain in Uganda*, 1932

Mair, L. P., *An African People in the 20th century (Buganda)*, 1934

Thomas, H. B., and Scott, R., *Uganda*, 1935

O'Brien, T. P., *Prehistory of the Uganda Protectorate*, 1939

Joelson, F. S., *Tanganyika Territory*, 1920

Orde-Browne, G. J., *Labour in Tanganyika*, 1926

Reid, E., *Tanganyika without Prejudice*, 1934

Richter, D. J., *Tanganyika and its Future*, 1934

Alexander, G., *Tanganyika Memories*, 1936

Cameron, Sir D., *My Tanganyika Service*, 1938

Raum, O. F., *Chaga Childhood*, 1940

Wood, A., *The Groundnut Affair*, 1951

Malcolm, D. W., *Sukamaland*, 1954

Smith, Rev. E. W., and Dale, A. M., *Ila-Speaking Peoples of N. Rhodesia* (2 vols.), 1930

Hole, H. M., *The Making of Rhodesia*, 1926

Meik, V., *Zambesi Interlude*, 1936

Robertson, W., *Zambesi Days*, 1936

Orde-Browne, G. J., *Labour Conditions in N. Rhodesia*, 1938

Richards, A. I., *Land, Labour and Diet in N. Rhodesia*, 1939

Johnson, W. P., *Nyasa, the Great Water*, 1922

Savile, F., *The High Grass Trail*, 1924

Norman, L. S., *Nyasaland without Prejudice*, 1934

Maugham, R. C. F., *Nyasaland in the Nineties*, 1936

Ingrams, W. H., *Zanzibar; its History and its People*, 1931

Pim, Sir A., *Finances and Economics of Zanzibar*, 1932

Crofton, R. H., *The Old Consulate at Zanzibar*, 1936

Newman, E. W. P., *Britain and North East Africa*, 1940

Rayne, H., *Sun, Sand and Somalis*, 1921
Drake-Brockman, R. E., *British Somaliland*, 1932
Hole, H. M., *Passing of the Black Kings*, 1933
Pim, Sir A., *Economic Conditions in the S. African Protectorates, 1933–5*
Curtis, L., and Perham, M., *The Protectorates of South Africa*, 1937
Merwick, B. A., *The Swazi; and Ethnographic study*, 1940
Schapera, L., *Married Life in an African Tribe*, 1940
Sillery, A., *The Bechuana Protectorate*, 1952
Paton, J. L., *Cry, the Beloved Country*, 1952
Brookes, E., *South Africa in a Changing World*, 1953
Dugmore, A. A., *The Vast Sudan*, 1924
Seligman, C. D. and B., *Pagan Tribes of the Nilotic Sudan*, 1932
Crabites, P., *The Winning of the Sudan*, 1934
Hamilton, J. A. de C., *The Sudan from Within*, 1937
Evans-Pritchard, E., *The Nuer*, 1940
MacMichael, Sir H., *The Sudan*, 1954

MEDITERRANEAN AND INDIAN OCEANS

Newman, E. W. P., *The Mediterranean and its Problems*, 1927
Wilson, Sir A., *The Suez Canal, Past, Present and Future*, 1934
Martellie, G., *Whose Sea?*, 1939
Williams, K., *Britain in the Mediterranean*, 1939
East, G., *Mediterranean Problems*, 1940
Garratt, G. T., *Gibraltar and the Mediterranean*, 1939
Howes, H. W., *Story of Gibraltar*, 1947
Zammit, Sir T., *Malta, the islands and their History*, 1926
Gatt, J. E. H., *Guide to Gozo*, 1927
Luke, Sir H., *Malta*, 1951
Peto. G. E., *Malta and Cyprus*, 1927
Storrs, Sir R., and O'Brien, *Handbook of Cyprus*, 1930
Knittel, R., *Cyprus Wine from my Cellar*, 1933
Gunnis, R., *Historic Cyprus*, 1936
Chapman, O. M., *Across Cyprus*, 1937
Casson, S., *Ancient Cyprus*, 1937
Hill, Sir G., *History of Cyprus*, 1940
Ingrams, W. H., *Social, Economic and Political Conditions of the Hadhramaut*, 1937
Stark, Freya, *Seen in the Hadhramaut*, 1939
Ireland, P. W., *Iraq; a study in Political Development*, 1938
Bailey, Sydney D., *Ceylon*, 1952
Monk, W. F., *Britain in the Western Mediterranean*, 1953

MAURITIUS, SEYCHELLES AND MALDIVES

Philogene, R., *The Island of Mauritius*, 1928
Toussaint, A., *Port-Louis; Deux Siecles d'Histoire*, 1937
Reid, T., *Financial Situation in the Seychelles*, 1934
Bradley, J. T., *History of the Seychelles Islands*, 1937
Ozanne, E., *Coconuts and Creoles*, 1937
Hockley, T. W., *The Two Thousand Isles (Maldives)*, 1935

MALAYA AND THE EAST

Makepeace, Brock and Braddell, *Hundred Years of Singapore* (2 vols.) 1921
Winstedt, Sir R., *Malaya*, 1923, *Malaya and its History*, latest edition, 1953
Gibson, A., *The Malay Peninsula and Archipelago*, 1928
Swettenham, Sir F., *British Malaya*, 1929
Bilainkin, G., *Hail, Penang*, 1933
Braddell, R., *The Lights of Singapore*, 1934
Ainsworth, L., *Confessions of a Planter in Malaya*, 1934
Foran, W. R., *Malayan Symphony*, 1935
Burkill, I. H., *Economic Products of the Malay Peninsula* (2 vols.), 1935
Lockhart, R. B., *Return to Malaya*, 1936
Fauconnier, H., *The Soul of Malaya*, 1937
Middlebrook, S. M. and Pinnick, *How Malaya is Governed*, 1940
Purcell, V., *The Chinese in Malaya*, 1948
Rutter, E. O., *British North Borneo*, 1922
Harrison, T., *Borneo Jungle*, 1939
Sarawak, Ranee Margaret, *My Life in Sarawak*, 1913; *Good Morning and Good Night*, 1935
Sarawak, Ranee Sylvia, *Three White Rajahs*, 1939
Keith, A., *Land below the Wind*, 1940
Sayer, G. R., *Hong Kong, Birth, Adolescence and Coming of Age*, 1937
Macdonald, T., *The Peak*, 1941
Ingrams, H., *Hong Kong*, 1951

THE PACIFIC ISLANDS

St. Johnston, Sir T., *Islands of the Pacific*, 1921; *South Sea Reminiscences*, 1922
Puxley, W. L., *Green Islands in the Glittering Sea*, 1925
Brown, J. M., *Peoples and Problems of the Pacific*, 1927

Ivens, W. G., *The Island Builders of the Pacific*
Cheesman, E., *Backwaters of the Savage South Seas*, 1933
Bellamy, R. R., *The Real South Seas*, 1933
Beaglehole, J. C., *Exploration of the Pacific*, 1934
Keesing, F. M., *Native Peoples of the Pacific*, 1934
Hogbin, H. I., *Law and Order in Polynesia*, 1934
Cromer, J., *Jock of the Islands*, 1935
Bernatzyk, H. A., *Sudsee; Travels in the South Seas*, 1935
Andrews, C. F., *India and the Pacific*, 1937
Grimble, Sir. A., *A Pattern of Islands*, 1952
Humphreys, C. B., *The Southern New Hebrides*, 1926
Harrisson, T., *Savage Civilization*, 1935
Marshall, A. J., *The Black Musketeers*, 1937
Wood, A. H., *History and Geography of Tonga*, 1932
Nordhoff and Hall, *Mutiny, Men against the Sea, Pitcairn Island* (3 vols.), 1935
Shapire, Dr. H. L., *Heritage of the Bounty*, 1936
Dickinson, J. H. C., *A Trader in the Savage Solomons*, 1927
Knibbs, S. C. G., *The Savage Solomons*, 1929
Firth, R., *Primitive Polynesian Economy*, 1939
Hogbin, H. I., *Experiments in Civilization*, 1940
Phillips, J. S., *Coconut Quest*, 1940
Miller, H., *New Zealand*, 1951

COMMONWEALTH DEPENDENCIES

Champion, I. F., *Across New Guinea from Fly to Sepik*, 1932
Monckton, C. A., *New Guinea Recollections*, 1934
Keesing, F. M., *Modern Samoa, its Government and Changing Life*, 1934
Cheesman, E., *Two Roads of Papua*, 1935
Hidea, J. G., *Through Wildest Papua*, 1935; *Papuan Wonderland*, 1936
Demaitre, D., *New Guinea Gold*, 1936
Leahy, M., and Grain, M., *The Land that Time Forgot*, 1939
Vedder, Dr. H., *South West Africa in Early Times*, 1939

FOREIGN COLONIES

Schase, Dr. H., *German Colonization*, 1926
Fraser, D. C., *Through the Congo Basin*, 1927
Jaspert, W., *Through Unknown Africa (Portuguese West)*, 1930
Roberts, W., *History of French Colonial Policy* (2 vols.), 1932

Sarrant, A., *Grandeur at Servitude Coloniale*, 1932
Tansill, C. C., *Purchase of the Danish West Indies*, 1932
Labouret, H., *Le Cameroun*, 1937
Roosevelt, T., *Colonial Policies of the U.S.A.*, 1937
Mumford and Orde-Brown, *Africans Learn to be French*, 1937
Howe, S. F., *The Drama of Madagascar*, 1938
Amery, L. S., *Germany's Colonial Claims*, 1939
Whybrow, S. J., and Edwards, H. E., *Europe Overseas*, 1939
Le Neveu, C. A., *Les Empires Colonaiux*, 1939
Pick, F. W., *Searchlight on German Africa*, 1940
Moore, M., *Fourth Shore (Italian Libya)*, 1940
Hollis, C., *Italy in Africa*, 1941

SOME BIOGRAPHIES

Harlow, V., *Christopher Codrington*, 1928
Smith, Rev. E. J., *Aggrey of Africa*, 1929
Maurois, A., *Marshal Lyautey*, 1931
Gwynn, S., *Life of Mary Kingsley*, 1932
Lockhart, J. G., *Cecil Rhodes*, 1932
Allen, B. M., *Gordon of the Sudan*, 1932
Megroz, R. L., *Ronald Ross; Discoverer and Creator*, 1932
Symons, A. J. A., *Henry M. Stanley*, 1933
Warner, A., *Sir Thomas Warner, a Pioneer of the West Indies*, 1934
Coupland, Sir R., *Raffles, 1781–1826*, 1934
Wellesley, D., *Sir George Goldie, Founder of Nigeria*, 1934
Gwynn, S., *Mungo Park and the Niger*, 1935
Gould, R. T., *Captain Cook*, 1935
Cruickshank, E. A., *Life of Sir Henry Morgan*, 1935
Huxley, Elspeth, *Lord Delamere (White Man's Country)* (2 vols.), 1935
Somervell, D. C., *Livingstone*, 1936
Lyne, R. N., *Apostle of Empire; Mathews of Zanzibar*, 1936
Dixon, C. W., *Colonial Administration of Sir Thos. Maitland*, 1940
Burns, Sir A., *Colonial Civil Servant*, 1950
Halson, L., *James Brooke of Sarawak*, 1953.
Perham, M., *Lord Lugard* (in preparation)

POSTSCRIPT

EVEN since this book was begun changes have taken place and events have happened, but fortunately it has been possible to anticipate or indicate most of them in the text. Under the new style of Crown Agents for Oversea Authorities and Administrations, that organization will continue its useful career. The Colonial Service is now to be known as the Overseas Service, and it can only be a question of time before "Colonial" disappears even from the title of the Colonial Office and of its responsible Minister. Sir Keith Hancock has successfully concluded his constitutional mission in Uganda, though the Kabaka is still exiled. Malta has not yet passed under the Home Office, but some closer bond will be devised. The Cyprus question has been deplorably handled, and Greece has brought it before the United Nations, a situation that should never have arisen. Agreement has been reached with Egypt as to the evacuation of the Suez base. The war in Indo-China has been settled and agreement reached for a South-East Asia treaty organization. The Gold Coast and Nigeria march steadily towards independence within the Commonwealth, but their new status and that of others in time will have to be agreed by the present members and that raises larger questions. And so events will continue to march, perhaps at an increasing pace, but the broad outline and framework of the Emergent Commonwealth as described in this book, and of the Commonwealth as a whole, remains true and as permanent as any human institution still in process of growth and development can be.

September 1954

INDEX

INDEX

A

Aden, 87
Africa, East and Central, 59
—— West, 47, 56
African Continent, 44, 77

B

Bahamas, 35
Barbados, 28
Basutoland, 75
Bechuanaland, 74
Bermuda, 36
Borneo, 99
British Guiana, 33
—— Honduras, 32
—— North Borneo, 101
—— Solomons, 107
—— Somaliland, 72
Broadcasting, 152
Brunei, 99

C

Caribbean and Atlantic Colonies, 24
Central African Federation, 67
—— machinery of government, 113, 131
Co-operation, 158
Colonial audit, 124
—— Council, 166
—— Government & Service, 126
—— Office, 114
—— policy and problems, 139
—— trade, 164
Colonies grow up, 16
Colour question, 155
Commonwealth Office, Greater, 166
Crown colony government, 128
—— Agents, 119
Cyprus, 84

E

Education, 151
Empire into Commonwealth, 9

F

Falkland islands, 41
Fiji, 104
Future trends, 160

G

Gambia, 47
Gibraltar, 79
Gilbert & Ellice group, 107
Gold Coast, 49

H

Health and disease, 146
High Commission territories, 73
Hong Kong, 101

I

Imperial Institute, 167

J

Jamaica, 26

K

Kenya, 60

L

Leeward islands, 29
Living standards, 144
Local government, 158

M

Malaya, 93
Maldives, 91
Malta, 81
Mauritius, 88
Mediterranean colonies, 79

INDEX

N

Nauru, 110
New Hebrides, 111
Nigeria, 52
Nutrition, 146
Nyasaland, 71

O

Official publications, 170
Overseas Service, 131

P

Pacific islands, 104
Periodicals, 169
Pests and diseases, 148
Phoenix group, 109
Pioneers, Colonial, 136
Pitcairn, 110

R

Rhodesias, North and South, 68

S

St. Helena and Ascension, 39
Sarawak, 93
Self-government, 139 *et passim*
Seychelles, 90
Sierra Leone, 48
Singapore, 96
Societies, empire and colonial, 137
Soil erosion, 150
South African protectorates, 73
Statute of Westminster, 13
Students questions, 155
Sudan, 57
Swaziland, 76

T

Tanganyika, 66
Tonga, 108
Trade unions, 158
Trinidad and Tobago, 27
Tristan da Cunha, 40
Trusteeship, 139 *et passim*

U

Uganda, 64

W

West Indies, 24, 37
Windward Islands, 31

Z

Zanzibar, 59

SELECTED LIST OF BOOKS AVAILABLE IN THIS SERIES

Starred titles 7s. 6d., unstarred 8s. 6d.

AUSTRALIA
R. M. CRAWFORD
(*Professor of History, University of Melbourne*)

*THE BRITISH WEST INDIES
W. L. BURN
(*Professor of Modern History, King's College, University of Durham*)

*BURMA
D. G. E. HALL
(*Professor of the History of South-East Asia in the University of London*)

*CANADA
G. S. GRAHAM
(*Rhodes Professor of Imperial History, University of London, formerly Professor of History, Queen's University, Canada*)

CEYLON
SYDNEY D. BAILEY
(*Assistant Director of the Hansard Society*)

*INDIA
C. H. PHILIPS
(*Professor of Oriental History in the University of London*)

MALAYA AND ITS HISTORY
SIR RICHARD WINSTEDT
(*Formerly of the Malayan Civil Service and Reader in Malaya in the University of London*)

NEW ZEALAND
HAROLD MILLER
(*Librarian of Victoria University College, Wellington, New Zealand*)

SOUTH AFRICA
ARTHUR KEPPEL-JONES
(*Senior Lecturer in History at the University of the Witwatersrand*)

BRITAIN IN THE WESTERN MEDITERRANEAN
W. F. MONK
(*Late Senior History Lecturer, Victoria University College, New Zealand*)

*THE WORLD CO-OPERATIVE MOVEMENT
MARGARET DIGBY
(*Secretary of the Horace Plunkett Foundation*)

THE BRITISH CO-OPERATIVE MOVEMENT
J. BAILEY
(*National Secretary of the Co-operative Party*)　(*Ready* 1955)

THE GOVERNMENT OF BRITAIN
WILFRID HARRISON
(*Fellow of Queen's College, Oxford*)

*TOWN AND COUNTRY PLANNING
M. P. FOGARTY
(*Professor of Industrial Relations, University of Wales, Fellow of Nuffield College, Oxford*)

POLITICAL THEORY
CHARLES VEREKER
(*Lecturer in Social and Political Theory, University of Liverpool*)　(*Due* 1955 *or* 1956)

THE STUDY OF POLITICAL BEHAVIOUR
D. E. BUTLER
(*Fellow of Nuffield College, Oxford*)　(*Ready* 1956)

*SOCIALISM
A Short History
NORMAN MACKENZIE
(Assistant Editor, *New Statesman and Nation*)

SOVIET RUSSIA
An Introduction
JACOB MILLER
(*Lecturer in Soviet Social and Economic Institutions, University of Glasgow, Joint Editor of 'Soviet Studies'*)
(*Ready Jan.* 1955)

THE STATE AND THE CITIZEN
An Introduction to Political Philosophy
J. D. MABBOTT
(*Fellow and Tutor of St. John's College, Oxford and University Lecturer in Philosophy*)

THE BRITISH STATUTE BOOK
C. J. HUGHES
Author of 'The Swiss Federal Constitution' (*Ready* 1956)

THE BRITISH EDUCATIONAL SYSTEM
G. A. N. LOWNDES (*Ready late* 1955)

THE RISE OF THE WAGE WORKER
E. J. HOBSBAWM
(*Lecturer in History, Birkbeck College, University of London, Ehrman Fellow of King's College, Cambridge*) (*Ready* 1956)

LABOUR
P. SARGENT FLORENCE
(*Professor of Commerce and Dean of the Faculty of Commerce and Social Science, University of Birmingham*)

SOCIAL PSYCHOLOGY AND INDIVIDUAL VALUES
D. W. HARDING
(*Professor of Psychology in the University of London*)

*SOCIOLOGY
W. J. H. SPROTT
(*Professor of Philosophy in the University of Nottingham*)

*SOCIAL SURVEYS
D. CARADOG JONES
(*Formerly Reader in Social Studies in the University of Liverpool*)

*COMPARATIVE LOCAL GOVERNMENT
G. MONTAGU HARRIS
(*Late President of the International Union of Local Authorities*)

*BRITISH LOCAL GOVERNMENT
E. C. R. HADFIELD and JAMES E. MACCOLL, J.P.
Mayor of Paddington, 1947–9

TRADE UNIONS
ALLAN FLANDERS
(*Senior Lecturer in Industrial Relations, University of Oxford*)

*DISTRIBUTIVE TRADING
An Economic Analysis
MARGARET HALL
(*Fellow and Tutor in Economics, Somerville College, Oxford*)

THE BRITISH BANKING MECHANISM
W. MANNING DACEY
(*Economic Adviser, Lloyds Bank*)

THE BRITISH COMMONWEALTH OF NATIONS
SIR IVOR JENNINGS, Q.C.
(*Master of Trinity Hall, Cambridge*)

A COMPLETELY REVISED EDITION READY LATE 1954